Plunge!

.

Plunge!

Sally Stiles

PeaCoat Press

PeaCoat Press
First Edition
Copyright © 2013 Sally Stiles

This story is written from memory, which is often capricious and always contorted by time. The excerpts from letters, telexes, audio tapes and books are virtually verbatim. Dialog, descriptions and scenes are carefully-rendered representations.

With gratitude to Bruce McAllister, Brian Curpier, Leland Lynch, Shelley Stiles Roeder, Patricia Wareing and Steven Roeder who have provided me permission to publish the scenes in which they appear.

I researched the facts and followed the sequence of events as nearly as possible. If any one of the many people mentioned in this book were to tell this story, it would become their story—and I would be eagerly listening to every word. I suspect they would offer variations and affirmations, additions and eliminations, but in the end, the essence of the story would remain the same.

Library of Congress Control Number: 2013910449
ISBN: 9781939917003

Marketed by PaleHorse Books
www.PaleHorseBooks.com

For David

"And then, thought Clarissa Dalloway, what a morning—fresh as if issued to children on a beach.
   "What a lark! What a plunge! For so it had always seemed to her, when, with a little squeak of the hinges, which she could hear now, she had burst open the French windows and plunged . . . into the open air . . . . Peter Walsh . . .would be back from India one of these days, June or July, she forgot which . . . it was his sayings one remembered; his eyes, his pocket-knife, his smile, his grumpiness and, when millions of things had utterly vanished—how strange it was!—a few sayings . . . ."
—Virginia Woolf, *Mrs. Dalloway*

Chapter One

For half a lifetime
I've wanted to record
who we were,
who we became—
examine, extrapolate, expound, explain,
and most of all
bequeath

but each story, poem
was just a scrap
overwritten by
the next day's verse,
the fresh ink vibrant,
paper crisp—

only now,
after the ending,
only now,
the ink running dry,
only now
the story begins

At thirty-two I knew all about love—what love
wasn't and was. Love could not be devised, not
demanded; did not conform to preconceptions.
Love could not be carved in granite to last forever, or even in pine to last a lifetime. Love was
an azure balloon, alluring, a fleeting wonder

which, with little warning, would twitch and fly away.

Though many years have passed, and love has now soared just beyond my reach, I still yearn to see, to smell, to rub my hand across that azure balloon.

When love seems farthest away, I revisit an extraordinary time when I was willing to travel half way around the world trailing after love. I listen to David's soft voice from a tape he recorded thirty-five years ago. "I want to tell you, so you can hear it, rather than reading it, how much I love you." There is a catch in his voice that tells me he means what he is saying. "I love you, I really do, and I can't wait until the day when we can begin our life together."

At this point in the tape—at this moment of promise—I want to start the story. But since the past always clings to the present; since it takes both past and present to create a whole story, at least one which makes any sense, I retreat to an earlier time before I'd even met David. From there the story will flow, as it must, like a muddying river headed toward a distant sea, filtering out debris to surge swiftly down narrow channels—then to slow, to even backtrack around the significant bends.

Chapter Two

Fly
a little while:
drift,
coast,
glide,
ascend,
descend—
land—
a thud so hard
my teeth
slap together.

Easy, easy
push the throttle,
easy, easy
airborne again,
in the pattern
praying—
please, God, please
next time you drop
me from the sky,
won't you do it gently?

The afternoon of July 11, 1974, I was in
California, flying over the ocean, performing
loops and rolls in an open-cockpit PT Stearman
biplane. What began as a demonstration ride

turned into an hour's instruction which stretched into two hours. I pushed the stick far right until I was upside down, watching white-caps roll over themselves, appearing to spin backwards. Then I pushed the stick again, and the plane rolled upright. I flew adjacent to the coast, straight and level, then goaded the nose toward the sun—higher, higher until the plane surged through a gentle backward loop and re-turned to level flight. I was somersaulting through the air—agile, free. This was *really, really* fun. This was ecstasy.

After we landed, I felt very much like my own hero. But when I returned to my hotel, the woman at the front desk handed me a message with a telephone number to call. It was the phone in a room at New York Presbyterian Hospital. I dialed it, and PK's sister, Nevart, answered. She told me PK was being monitored; he may have had a heart attack.

PK—his initials easier for Americans to pronounce than his name—was a charming, light-hearted, never-married fifty-one year-old Egyptian-Armenian, flecks of gray in his mustache. I was twenty years younger. Our mostly on-again relationship had endured for nearly ten years.

I caught the red-eye out of San Diego and spent a nervous night in the air, praying that PK would be alive by the time I reached New York. I tried to concentrate on the jumbled notes for the story I was writing for *Flying* Magazine, and then on the book I had picked up in the airport, Erica Jong's *Fear of Flying*. The novel seemed neither erotic nor funny, as the reviews promised. When I deplaned, I left it under my seat.

After arriving at JFK the next morning, I went straight to the hospital. PK was doing well, so well they released him late that afternoon, and Nevart and I brought him to his apartment. She and his elderly mother stayed with him, and I reluctantly went home to unpack.

As I leaned down to kiss him good-bye, he looked at me with curiosity, as if he were seeing me for the first time.

"Sally," he said, "take care of yourself."

"Shouldn't I be saying that to you?" I laughed. "I'll see you in the morning."

I willed myself into bed, having not slept for the past thirty-six hours, yet woke up time and again throughout the night from an ever-more vexing dream: PK was on the far side of a gorge, walking away from me down a narrow path. I would lose sight of him if I could not find a bridge. I ran through the thick clusters of brush and trees along the gorge, but there was no bridge.

I woke up, fell asleep, still searching for the bridge. Then he turned down an alley on the other side of a six-lane highway where racing cars rushed past—red, blue and yellow racing cars—each with a number painted on an oval on the driver's door: one, forty-nine, twelve. There was no way to cross between the cars to reach him.

When I next awoke, early on Saturday morning, I dressed hurriedly in hip-hugging bell-bottom jeans and a pink cotton jersey and took the Lexington Avenue IRT uptown and walked across 59th Street past Columbus Circle to PK's apartment. He was tired but in good spirits. We talked awhile until he fell asleep on the couch. I picked up the book beside him and began to read: Bertrand Russell's *Portraits from Memories*.

Nevart put together a grocery list, and I went out to Gristedes. When I returned, she retired to the bedroom to take a nap, and his mother retreated to the kitchen to make *yalanchi sarma*. The sweet smell of lamb and mint emanated from the kitchen; PK woke up, and, again, I sat down beside him. With his eyelids still half closed, he joked with me: "You ran off to the West and cracked my heart—but at least it didn't stop beating."

He grinned, his smile lopsided as always—a little higher on the right side where his cheek dimpled. I brushed his face with my hand, relieved he had gotten through this. He would be okay; we would be okay. There was no gorge; no racing cars tearing down a highway to separate us.

But then he took my hand, and, in his appealing Middle-Eastern accent, sounding almost as if he were translating, slowly said, "My brother died of a heart attack when he was younger than I am now. I could have a stroke and be incapacitated. It wouldn't be fair to you to have to take care of an old, sick man. You are still young."

Though I understood what I was hearing, I refused to believe his health could break even the most fragile of links that connected us. I still

6

assumed that, when the time was right, we would be married.

"You don't have to worry," I said. "I take vows seriously: for better or worse; in sickness and in health. I wouldn't leave you." His large, dark eyes seem troubled.

He turned his head from me to watch a gray pigeon land on the window sill. The Pigeon hopped along the ledge then stopped and furtively, nervously examined us through the hazy window.

"Look at me," I said. "Doesn't love mean anything to you?"

I thought he might return an angry retort, but, instead, he looked at me then with tenderness—such tenderness and such longing—I could not take my eyes from his. "Don't make this any harder," he said. "You have so much more to experience than I have left to offer."

"No, don't say that. Don't give up on us. We still have years of life to experience together."

He raised a finely-shaped, manicured hand, clenched and unclenched his fist, then slowly dropped his hand to his lap. He closed his eyes and soon was asleep again.

Late that afternoon, still feeling the effects of jet lag from my coast-to-coast trip, tired from the previous night of little sleep and knowing PK needed rest, I kissed him good night and left his apartment. A few hours later we talked on the phone. As we ended the call, we said "I love you" at the same time. Then we said "good night"— again at the same time. We laughed. We did not say good-bye.

I would see him in the morning. I would convince him that I could take care of him, and he would become healthy again. We'd plan a relaxing trip to Bermuda. We'd walk on pink sand beaches and float in warm, turquoise water. I would not let him give up.

Within an hour his sister telephoned me: "PK's collapsed!"

The streets were steaming from a short but intense rain shower, and no taxis were in sight. I waved frantically, and finally an old, dark blue Ford Fairlane slowed down beside my building at Park and 35th.

"Hey," the driver yelled out. "You need to go somewhere?"

I opened the back door and peered inside. Some Gypsy cabs had meters; some did not. There was no meter in this car. "Oh, shit," I said. "I thought you might be a metered cab."

I looked up and down Park Avenue, but there were no taxis coming in either direction.

"Look," he said. "I'm not a taxi driver. I'm just on my way uptown. And you looked really desperate for a ride. So where do you need to go?"

"I just got a call. My boyfriend. He's—I don't know. He may have had a heart attack. I need to get to him right away."

"Where does he live?"

"Columbus Circle. Near there."

"No problem," he said. "I'll take you."

"Really? You'd do that?" I asked. "Would $10 be enough?"

"Just get in."

I sat on the edge of the rear seat behind the driver, my hand on the door handle in case I needed to escape in a hurry. I had no idea who this young man was; all I could see of him was greasy brown hair curling below his collar and the outline of his black-rimmed glasses; I only knew I had to get to PK—fast.

As he drove up Park Avenue, I told him about PK being in the hospital and about the phone call from PK's sister. I said I didn't know if PK would still be at home when I arrived, or if he would have been taken to Roosevelt, the nearest hospital.

"We'll be there in a couple of minutes," he said to reassure me. "The medics will be with him, and everything will be okay."

As we neared 57th Street, he asked me for the address. By this time, I figured I had nothing to lose, and, indeed, he delivered me safely to the sidewalk in front of PK's building. A police car was parked just ahead of us. There was nobody inside, and no lights were flashing. "Please, God, please. Just let PK be okay."

Through the open window on the driver's side, I pressed $10 into the young man's hand. He shook his head and handed it back. I dropped the money on his lap and thanked him; told him he was a Good Samaritan. "You'll go to heaven," I said, then ran from the car into the building.

The tall Jamaican doorman looked worried as he pushed open the glass door. I rushed past him and raced down the hall to the elevator. Both cars appeared to be stuck on the top floor where Mitch Miller, the sing-along TV host, lived.

I ran around the corner and dashed up five flights and knocked on the door while inserting my key. A young, wiry policeman opened the door. I looked into his face, stern, unsmiling, and then I looked beyond him. Nevart and PK's mother were sitting on the couch, his sister crying, his mother weeping into a handkerchief covering her face. On the floor just left of the door what remained of PK was sealed within a black body bag. I skirted around the policeman, hugged PK's mother, then his sister, then knelt beside the bag and shuddered, as close as I had ever been to death.

It happened so fast that I was stunned. I was on the phone, talking to PK. I was getting ready for bed. Nevart called. I raced uptown. PK was gone. How long had he lived after I spoke to him? After we had laughed together?

I tried to envision PK inside the bulky sack, but could not bring up his face. Was he smiling or grimacing; did he look astounded, or was he simply vacant, beyond peace? I imagined him wearing his pin-striped suit, the burgundy vest, a matching handkerchief neatly folded in his suit pocket, though more likely he was in his laundered and carefully pressed pale blue pajamas, the same pajamas he wore when I left him that afternoon. What were his last thoughts, what words?

Earlier that afternoon, was PK trying to tell me he was dying? Were last night's dreams portents of his death? Was I not paying attention? And hadn't I said I would never leave him? Yet I had gone away and fantasized about helping him become whole again. And now he was gone.

Gone was my affectionate companion, a bright, inquisitive man with whom I had shared Saturday afternoons in Central Park, Sundays with the *New York Times*, museum exhibits, Broadway shows, Nixon's resignation, the Apollo moon landing which we watched from a fuzzy black and white television in his family's cabin on Lake George.

The man whose body fit pleasingly next to mine was gone. A fascinating man, mysterious, enchantingly exotic, a man old enough to have been the father I all but lost at age five—a man I thought I loved was gone, and gone with him were his stories of the Nile and the Pyramids, his backyard as a young man; stories about his relatives fleeing Turkey with jewelry sewn into their clothing.

Gone was the man who tossed back his head to laugh with abandon; who showed me how to play backgammon and how to make *tahnabour*, a yogurt soup; gone was the man who taught me how to become a woman, though not enough, perhaps, about how to love.

I met him at a typical New York party, the women seeming to me that night to be overly animated and the men unconvincingly cool. He was sitting alone on a couch, attentive to the scene unfolding before him. I sat beside him, and we began to talk. He had traveled and worked in interesting places, most recently Japan. I wanted to hear more, so I accepted his invitation for dinner. Within a few minutes we left the party and

11

went around the corner to Ararat, an Armenian restaurant, where he introduced me to grape leaves and baklava.

Throughout all our tumultuous years together, when I most felt his lack of commitment, I had dated other men, some of them unwise choices, some acceptable though dull. Each time I returned to PK. Each time he welcomed, or even lured me back.

◆

The undertaker came; they lifted PK onto a gurney and took him away. I stood at the window watching below as they slid him into the black hearse. And then, for the first time since I arrived, I felt my tears release and stream silently down my cheeks.

His mother and sister had not moved from the couch. I went over to his mother and took the handkerchief from her hand. I wiped her face, brushed back loose strands of hair which had escaped her grey chignon, and she was still for a moment. Then she sobbed and held her arms across her heavy breasts and breathed in short, strident, labored breaths. She began to gulp for air. When her breathing did not improve I called down to the doorman to fetch us a cab to take us the few blocks to the emergency room of Roosevelt hospital. His sister stayed behind to notify family members.

After an interminable wait in the callous green light of the waiting room, where I held his mother's hand and tried to keep her calm, we were ushered into a treatment room, and, as his mother spoke little English, I told the attending doctor what had happened and what little I knew of her medical history. He examined her, gave her a sedative and sent her home to her son's empty bed. In the early hours of the morning, with his mother asleep and breathing normally and his sister in her nightclothes under sheets on the couch, I left the apartment.

On my way home in the cab I wondered, as I wonder now, what I really meant to PK. Maybe he saw me as a caring life companion for whom he'd once bought a wedding band which he declined to bless with marriage vows. Maybe I was the love of his life, or maybe not. But for a long time I knew I would hold him in memory—hold him even closer than while he lived.

♦

The family wanted me to join them up front at the funeral. I chose to sit with his friends in the middle of church. The minister who gave the uninspired eulogy mispronounced his name.

Nightmares, depression and accompanying anxiety attacks began a week after the service. I agonized over whether or not I could have loved him more; if I might have saved him had I been in New York instead of California or had I stayed with him the evening he died. My brain began to swirl without my permission, like spinning paint: dark blue, deep purple, then yellow, then a numbing thump—dull gray.

Gone was the man who, on the day he died, had gazed at me with such compassion, such tenderness, while he broke my heart.

I kept functioning—working, editing, writing—but sometimes felt as if I were slogging through muck, each step harder than the last. At times I would come to an impasse, having no idea which way to turn, and a chill would crawl down my body. No doubt in my subconscious I was reliving the perplexing separation from another man twenty-seven years earlier. That man was my father.

On weekends through the rest of July and August, I often walked the city, though it was oppressively hot and abandoned except for the old, the poor and the demented.

On Sunday afternoons, when I walked down the broad sunlit avenues, I felt as if I were alone in an empty museum where the paraphernalia of insatiable city dwellers lay, as if preserved for posterity behind the windows of the closed stores: Halston sheets, Warhol prints, Capote books, Nureyev posters, Yves St. Laurent ties, Hermes scarves, Gucci bags.

One weekend I walked near the Bowery where a man and a woman lay across the subway grates, his beard glinting silver, thorny; their white skin too brown, as if bathed in formaldehyde.

Through Mulberry Street's garlic haze, a wild-haired woman leaned from a cracked third-story window and screamed in Italian at a filthy boy who was sobbing as he ran away from her into an alley. I wanted to grab the child, hold him

14

until his tears evaporated. I wanted to erase his fear.

On the Lower West Side piers, several dozen men in bikini bathing trunks lay on the hot boards, many in pairs. Their caressing saddened me, as I knew that behind each stroke was, in all probability, a story of denial then defiance, of fear and rejection. And we had not yet named the terrible disease that could kill any one of them at random for a single afternoon of bliss.

Once I meandered up Broadway to the Upper West Side where several fat men in undershirts sprawled across the stoops of brownstones, empty cans of Rheingold Beer scattered around their feet. They must have once desired something better.

I crossed 72nd Street and entered Central Park, and where the sun filtered through the trees, two teenagers held hands, a child tumbled on the grass, laughing, and, at the conservatory pond, a man showed his son how to sail a model boat—small flashes of joy, of hope.

Walking back through midtown, I passed a businessman who appeared to have come into the city a day early. He stopped and watched me walk by. I looked into his eyes, pale as bleached denim, then hurried past and turned down a side street before he could suggest I join him for a drink; I knew I did not have the strength nor the will to assuage his temporary loneliness.

Chapter Three

For my tenth birthday,
Mother's idea:
four tables, sixteen girls,
a gentle game
of hearts.

Fifteen girls playing safe,
shunning every heart,
the horrid Queen of Spades.
I, alone, tried to shoot the moon.

No matter what was dealt,
I tried to steal
every heart and the dirty lady.
Yes, a dangerous ploy.

No, I didn't win.
But I still craved
the elusive, the beguiling,
the utterly unattainable. The moon.

There are many reasons and many ways for people to leave home. The first time I left I was eight years old. I didn't run away but simply refused to go back. When I realized it was Thursday and Campfire Girl camp would end in two days, I went to the director's office.

"Miss Johnson, you need to call my mother," I said.

"What's the matter? Are you sick?" She peered down at me in my blue shorts, white button-down blouse, the requisite red kerchief looped around my neck. I looked hopefully into her kind, smiling face.

"Sally?"

"Yes ma'am?" She looked concerned. I plucked up all my courage.

"I'm not sick. Cross my heart. I just want—I don't want to go home yet."

I'd discovered that at camp I was expected to be a kid and was treated like a kid, so if I was silly or untidy or couldn't get the hang of the back jackknife dive, I might be encouraged to do better, but nobody seemed disappointed.

"Can't you please just call my mother and ask if I can stay?"

Miss Johnson looked perplexed. "What about your clothes? Your sheets? You brought enough for two weeks, and they'll need washing. And your mother will have to get us the money for another session."

"Yes ma'am." I pulled off the white sailor cap I always wore at camp and rolled it in my hands, then looked at her with all the earnestness I could muster. "If you lend me some soap, I can wash my clothes—maybe in the lake? And my mother will send you a check. I know she will! She'll be happy she doesn't have to worry about me. Please, please, can't I just stay? Becky, my counselor, she's *sooooo* nice. She said it would be okay—I mean if it's okay with you and you call my mother. I know my mother will let me stay."

Miss Johnson called my mother who drove up on the weekend with fresh sheets and clothes, and I stayed another two weeks.

◆

Through my sixteenth year, I escaped to one camp or another every summer, first as a camper and, beginning at age twelve, as a counselor. The summer before turning seventeen, I got on a train in Atlanta, headed for Chicago, changed to the Denver Zephyr, took a bus up into mountains and worked all summer at Meeker Park Lodge in Allenspark, Colorado. The next summer I did the same before going off to Ohio to college. After that, I never went back to Atlanta to live.

My mother felt girls should be trained as teachers or nurses to have a job to fall back upon when their marriage failed. Hers had failed, so she must have sadly assumed her children's marriages would fail as well. My sister, ten years my senior, was at Emory University, studying to be a nurse. I was expected to be a teacher. In the time, the place, Mother was acting like a conscientious parent. But the times were shifting, and I was moving faster than she could run to catch up with me.

Despite my mother's insistence on a safe career, I first entertained the idea of being a writer when Miss Jones, my fourth grade teacher, tacked one of my poems on the corkboard and never took it down. After that, my mother sometimes printed my naïve and crudely composed poems on her Christmas cards. Sometimes she'd use my older brother's poems. I felt then—and know now—that his were far superior.

Still, at thirteen, when I got home from school, I sometimes escaped into my bedroom to read *Seventeen* Magazine and learn what a successful teenager would wear, read, think and do. *National Geographic* took me across deserts, up mountains, through jungles and into distant cities. I began to dream of writing for a magazine, a desire too outsized, too significant, to be spoiled by being told it was an unattainable fantasy. Until I was a senior at Miami University in Ohio and made editor of the yearbook, I never spoke to anyone about my aspirations.

After college, I went to Boston for the Radcliffe College Publishing Program. On my way back to Atlanta for a friend's wedding, I stopped a couple of days in New York, staying at the YWCA and paying more to park my car than for my room. I applied at *McCall's* Magazine for an entry job posted on the bulletin board at Radcliffe. In front of Paul Cezanne's *The Card Players* at the Metropolitan Museum appeared Bonnie, a college friend willing to be a roommate. We leased a brand-new one-bedroom apartment on the far west side of Greenwich Village, and I was on my way to living my dream of working for a magazine.

I worked for McCall Corporation for a year, my co-workers not nearly so stimulating as my college friends. In less than a year, I had gone from discussing what seemed to be crucial philosophical and political topics and directing a large yearbook staff to a mundane job—typing letters, filing them and laying out mail order ads. My desk was the first of several in a row, those behind me occupied by high-school graduates from Brooklyn who had no interest in the crucial question of how Schopenhauer's view of the irrational universe had influenced Thomas Hardy or D.H. Lawrence.

Directly across the aisle in front of me was the boss, who swallowed a vast number of horehound drops from a glass dish on his desk and smirked like an overgrown, overweight tenth-grader.

While I endured my first job in New York for a year, occasionally, when I was overwhelmed with boredom, I pleaded temporary illness and escaped by subway to the Battery to catch a five-cent ride on the Staten Island Ferry. Returning by Liberty Island, the great lady with her raised lamp would invariably embolden me, and the next morning I would show up at my desk to try once again to prove my ability to rise in the world of magazine publishing.

Within a year, for a $2,000 (thirty percent) raise in salary, I joined Ziff-Davis Publishing Company to work at *Car & Driver*. I knew little about cars and had owned nothing grander than a turquoise Volkswagen Beetle, though in high school I had favored boys who owned Triumph TR3s and MG-As.

On a rainy night when I was seventeen, I was driving my mother's clunky Chevy Bel Air when Ted pulled up beside me in his TR3. We skirted around a barrier on Peachtree Street, lined up next to each other and raced down one of Atlanta's partially-constructed expressways. Ted won, but by the time I reached the end of the pavement, I knew that driving with my right foot to the floor demanded all my wits and was as exhilarating as it was scary. With our headlights off, we crept back to the barrier and turned onto Peachtree just before a police car passed us going the other way. I checked the rear-view mirror all the way home, afraid that I would be caught and arrested.

At *Car & Driver* I learned a good deal about automobiles under the raucous, irreverent tutelage of venerable automotive journalists David E. Davis, Jr. and Brock Yates, who was the brother-in-law of a college friend and had encouraged me to join the staff. While the office talk was still a long way from the questions we passionately considered in college, there were political and philosophical matters to discuss, provided they were sufficiently automotive: What categorical imperative motivated Ralph Nader to write *Unsafe at Any Speed?*

I wrote a few stories, wrote a lot of captions and edited a lot of manuscripts and drove some fun cars—like the Jaguar XKE outfitted with a Pontiac Hemi engine that overheated every seven miles.

A year later, having never even ridden a motorcycle, I graduated to *Cycle* magazine as an assistant editor, then moved up through the ranks, eventually as managing editor.

A few weeks after joining the staff I learned to ride a bike while posing as a motorcycle stunt rider, standing in for Ethel Merman in a TV production of *Annie Get Your Gun*. I was directed to maneuver a spindly red Moto Guzzi around in a circle and hold a rifle in my right hand, the throttle hand.

When I got on the bike, a burly motorcycle-wise stage hand who owned a Suzuki X-6 taped the throttle down. I rode a hundred feet, and the bike slipped out from under me. I dusted myself off, told the stage hand that learning how to fall was the first step in becoming a stunt rider, then got back on and, two takes later, left with the promise of a check for a much-needed $300 and had actually ridden a motorcycle.

The sequence cut between me and a close up of Ethel Merman on a stationary, papier-mâché mocked-up motorcycle. I always wondered how it looked, since Ethel Merman was a large woman at the time and I weighed 115 pounds. When it aired, I was in Daytona for bike week, having dinner with Grand National Champion Gary Nixon and his wife. Gary was a wiry, cocky Oklahoman who rode his 500cc Triumph with an unrestrained will to win, and spoke through his teeth, usually to challenge his competitors with a taunt like, "Which one of you guys is going to come in second?"

Besides editing articles, writing headlines and captions, and tediously assembling buyer's guides, I wrote many off-beat stories for the magazine, including reporting on the Quebec City Winter Carnival ice races—bike tires

23

studded with long, menacing spikes—and home-grown track racing in Wisconsin at the Door County fair.

The magazine requisitioned two small Honda 160s to test over a long period of time, and I claimed the road version as my own to travel throughout the city, occasionally on Sunday afternoon outings with Ivy-league executives who belonged to the Madison Avenue Motorcycle Club.

On our sporadic staff forays to the back woods of New Jersey, we would unload a bunch of dirt bikes and tear around the trails, the guys riding bigger and faster bikes than I did, and with greater abandon, though I still enjoyed launching off a bump and flying a few yards before touchdown.

In 1969, along with our duties at *Cycle*, Cook Neilson edited the first issue of *Invitation to Snowmobiling,* and I was the managing editor. Shortly afterwards, *Cycle* editor Gordon Jennings became editor of *Car & Driver*, Cook moved up to editor of *Cycle*; I received the consolation prize: the snowmobile magazine. And that was exactly the way it should have been.

I imagine that Cook was working at Ziff-Davis to write about motorcycles. I was there to write about anything they'd let me write about. My *Snowmobiling* stories—editorials, profiles, adventure features—provided the magazine's romance. The technical staff delivered the necessary nuts and bolts, including thorough test results on new sleds, and art director George

Ramos created award-winning spreads. The magazine was fun, bold, splashy—beautiful.

Throughout the winter months I had a chance to slide and glide a snowmobile over new-fallen snow, hanging out over the edge in power turns, gazing over the Tetons or the Rockies, or riding the trails along the St. Lawrence Seaway in Quebec.

My job took me on small feeder airlines hurtling through clear, starry nights to small-town airports in Minnesota, Wisconsin, Idaho, Ontario, Michigan's Upper Peninsula, where the plane would land on runways obscured by swirling, stinging snow. I went to conventions and factories and test sessions and races and met strange backwoods people, like a hermit who hid out in a cabin near Wenatchee, Washington, and Timber Jack Joe, last mountain man of the Rockies, a foul-smelling trapper who lived in a cluttered trailer with his dog, Tuffy, near Jackson, Wyoming.

Many a Saturday night, accompanied by various members of my staff or by public relations managers hoping for a story, I arrived at a VFW hall or roadside café to shoot pool and get to know the snowmobiling locals who drank Hamm's beer at the bar and danced in their wet boots and broad suspenders to the juke box wail of Tammy Wynette.

In 1971, I was invited by Bombardier, Inc. of Quebec to join a chartered flight from Vancouver, BC to Whitehorse in the Yukon. During most of the two-hour flight through the interior of British Columbia, vast stretches of barren land sprawled below us, and no lights glowed, making the journey seem much longer than it was. The Yukon encompasses more than 207,000 square miles of land, though, at that time, fewer than 25 miles of road were paved, making the dog sled and the new iron dog—the snowmobile—the preferred method of winter travel.

My assignment was to witness and write about the Sourdough Rendezvous, a three-day party with contests of strength and skill meant to relieve cabin fever and celebrate a break from the bitter January weather. By February in the town of Whitehorse, the thermometer averages a balmy 17 degrees, Fahrenheit.

I had such a good time and was so intrigued by the hearty, independent spirit of those who lived in the Klondike that, two years later, I invented an excuse to return. But this time I would attempt to snowmobile the 400-mile overland gold rush trail from Skagway, Alaska to Dawson in the Yukon.

In mid-March, 1973, a couple of trappers from Anchorage, their stuffed totem, Teddy, a photographer and I gathered in Haines, Alaska. We took over the local Ski-Doo shop to load up four snowmobiles with a thousand pounds of gear, then drove them up a ramp onto a truck to ferry them across the Upper Lynn Canal to Skagway. Some fifteen miles from the base of the Chilkoot Pass, where thousands of gold-hungry prospectors had crossed into the Yukon in 1898, we unloaded the sleds. Only then did we discover that only one snowmobile had yet reached the pass, and none had traversed it.

We mushed back and forth across the icy Dyea River, standing on the snowmobiles, plowing across the rocks, water spilling over the seats, then hauled the sleds when we couldn't ride them up the rutted, winding cliff-side trail which was often slick with glare ice. It took us three hours to reach the top of the first hill on the trail. Like the gold seekers before us, we lightened the loads and finally reached Sheep Camp, once a booming town where over a thousand miners would gather at any one time before tackling the Chilkoot Pass. Only one small Park Service cabin remained there.

At night in the cabin, with a pint of Canadian whiskey, the dense smell of smoke from the wood stove mingling with the tang of wet wool shirts hanging from the rafters, and the sound of wolves yowling in the distance, we played poker with home-made cards and took turns reading aloud from Pierre Berton's fine book, *Klondike Fever,* about the 1898 gold rush. Berton told us that an entrepreneur cut steps into the pass and charged for their use. Another recovered discarded hip waders from the Dyea River and sold them over and over again in Juneau. On St. Patrick's Day, we read that hundreds had died in an avalanche on April 3, 1898. Yet, undaunted, after breakfast the next morning we started out again for the summit.

For days, attempting a run over the top, we arose in below-zero weather, the wind blowing and snow drifting, ice balls clinging to our furry gloves and tuques. Each time, we failed to ascend the slope that rises a thousand feet in the final half mile. The snow was too soft and deep to hold the sleds, even at full throttle.

Ziff-Davis' only woman editor-in-chief was not a terrible choice for *Snowmobiling.* I edited it for four years, from age twenty-seven to thirty-one. Many years later a web post called my magazine (and it will always be *my* magazine) "the holy grail of sno-go publications." Reading such an accolade after so long a time felt nice. Very nice.

As I look back on those years, they meld into a memory that seems to belong to someone else's life. That late-night February ride in Thief River Falls, Minnesota when it was forty below: I wonder now what was I still trying to prove then.

◆

In the spring of 1974, Ziff-Davis sold my magazine for a reputed million dollars. I decided to freelance for a few months and wrote stories for a number of publications, including *Boating, Skiing* and *Popular Photography,* all published by Ziff-Davis.

While I was trying to figure out how I would survive in Manhattan without a monthly paycheck, my former boss and his wife, Chuck and Joy Curpier, both private pilots, convinced me to take a flight with Chuck's brother, Brian, an instructor and pilot for Catskill Airways in Oneonta, New York.

Brian pushed the throttle forward and the plane roared down the runway, then, as he pulled back on the wheel, the nose lifted and we were airborne.

I had spent hours on commercial flights, glued to the window beside me, and, time and again, had been juddered by the fearsome rumble of jet engines gaining enough power for takeoff. Each time, leaving the runway, I felt relief. That day, in the cockpit for the first time, I felt elation when we left the earth and headed toward the heavens.

To me, taking off in a small, private plane was astounding—like being in the fourth row at Carnegie Hall to hear a live symphony for the very first time, and after ten minutes of sitting next to Brian, I knew I wanted to become like him, completely at home in the skies.

He let me take the controls. With Brian's gentle coaching, I slowly brought the wheel back and pushed the throttle forward, and the Beechcraft 23 Sundowner began to ascend. He told me to try to hold the plane level at 5,000 feet. After a short while, the needle on the altimeter seemed reasonably steady. "Now hold your course on the compass at 330 degrees," he said. I glanced over at him. "And hold your altitude." He was smiling.

"Let's turn to 350 degrees," he said. I rotated the wheel so that the right wing dipped and the plane changed direction at my command. Two twenty-eight, two twenty-nine—whoops—two thirty two. I rotated the wheel back again—two twenty-nine. "And hold your altitude!" Again he smiled. I was both relieved and disappointed when he reclaimed the wheel; what I had just felt was akin to omnipotence. I was on top of the world, awkwardly but pleasurably manipulating a machine that could take me just about anywhere I wanted to go.

Incredibly, Brian made that airplane waltz. He flew up and up, the features of the land diminishing below us, then veered gently to the west and descended a thousand feet so I could see the Curpier farm below. He slowly wove around the billowing clouds to unveil the tranquil pastures beneath us, then we meandered gently, majestically, back to Earth.

After Brian landed, I signed up for my next lesson, jumped into my Fiat and rolled back the roof. Never mind the chilly mountain air; I wanted to look up at the sky. I laughed to myself all the way home. I'd just flown an airplane. Wow!

In May, Bob Parke of *Flying*, another Ziff-Davis publication, called and offered me a job. At the time, my experience in private planes was limited to two hour-long lessons. But I could edit, and I could write, and I couldn't wait to get back into an airplane to feel the exhilaration I had felt in the air with Brian.

I worked successfully in a man's world, on magazines predominantly read by men, publications for devoted enthusiasts, so it was my job to be equally passionate about cars, then bikes, then snowmobiles, then planes. Many of my male colleagues were wary of me, some verbally, since I didn't fit in any of the lidded containers created for women in the early '70s, and I was disappointed that they couldn't see me for who I was:

a hard-working woman with an interesting career. I wasn't a tough broad or a ball-breaker. Despite what some of them said, I shouldn't have been home ironing and cooking. Like my male counterparts and friends, I was a writer and an editor, intent on doing a good job.

Those were the days when women were standing, bewildered, at the trailhead of opportunity. Few had gone to law school or medical school; less than ten percent of MBA candidates were women. Helen Gurley Brown, editor of *Cosmopolitan*, was telling women to be sexually liberated and slightly stupid. *Ms* editor, Gloria Steinem, was telling women to be totally liberated and very bright. I wanted to be able to work my clever ass off and still emerge as a woman desired. If nothing else, how many women had the enviable access to the latest new cars, new bikes, new snowmobiles and new airplanes?

Some of my friends worked for Time-Life or the glossy fashion magazines published by Condé-Nast, and occasionally I considered trying to get a more dignified, more lady-like job with one of the larger magazines. Often I felt I should do something more serious with my life. But I was happy at Z-D even though—and because—it was a quirky, mostly fun place to work. Where else would your desk be situated between a gay former Marine and a cantor's son who had sewn a doorknob to his leather jacket? Where else would I learn so much about the world—about how companies operated, and how interesting people lived their lives? Where else would I have access to a subbasement darkroom to spend late hours trying to coax beautiful black and white images from my negatives, accompanied by the patter of rats scurrying in and out of the adjacent subway?

Above all, I cherished the creative freedom we editors generally enjoyed. We could go where we felt we needed to go to get a good story and write the truth as we understood it.

Before I was given a desk at *Flying*, I was sent to Florida to Flight Safety, the aeronautical school in Vero Beach. Under a tough former Air Force ace with a loud, gravelly voice, I discovered that, unlike Brian, not all pilots saw flight as a form of poetry. We performed precision climbs, turns, slow flight, stalls, touch and goes over and over again. My instructor was pushing me to solo in the minimum eight hours. I came back to New York after twelve hours of sharing a cockpit with him, still never having flown a plane alone, and wondering if I ever would. I felt that I had failed.

But on several weekends that summer I went up to Stewart Field in Newburgh, NY, for more flight instruction with a laid-back instructor. After the pre-flight check we'd get into the 140 Piper. He'd light up a cigarette, settle in, nod his head and tell me to take off. And quietly, almost sleepily, he'd put me through my paces.

Stewart Field was initially a training ground for the nearby military academy at West Point with runways long enough for jumbo jets—plenty of room for a student pilot to learn to land a two-seat Piper. I soloed at Stewart the first of September, 1974, and again a week later. Just before Thanksgiving, I made my first solo flight cross-country from Kobelt, a small, one-runway airport in Wallkill, NY to Waterbury-Oxford in Connecticut and back.

The distance between the two airports was 46 nautical miles. I would fly by dead reckoning, checking my progress by landmarks and holding fast to the compass heading, correcting only for wind speed and compass error. By then I had received only scant instrument training in automatic direction finders and VOR navigation—but enough to hopefully get me out of trouble if necessary.

I taxied down to the end of Runway 3-21 and took off over the trees on a heading of 210 degrees, then gained sufficient altitude and turned right to a heading of 296 degrees. After crossing the Hudson River and reaching an altitude of 3,000 feet, the flight would be direct and uncomplicated as I crossed the small rivers, lakes and expanses of trees across the Hudson River Valley. Up in the air, well beyond the airport for the first time with nobody beside me, unable to pull over and drag out the chart, I realized how daunting it was to fly. I felt anxious, yet all parts of my brain were running with the throttle wide open. I could, I would succeed.

Then came the glitch, an error to which no self-respecting pilot would ever admit, and even I refused to admit for years. I looked straight ahead and to my right and saw an airport, and was about to call the tower for permission to enter the landing pattern when it occurred to me that, unless an enormous tail wind had pushed me toward my destination, I wasn't there yet. I still had some fifteen or sixteen nautical miles to go. And Waterbury-Oxford had only one runway. This airport had two.

So where the hell was I? I checked the direction of the strip running parallel below me against my compass and the Sectional on the seat next to me. Two runways. One was below me at 260 degrees. I rechecked the chart. Danbury. I had to be nearing Danbury. I glanced quickly at the chart again. If I kept the same heading, Waterbury-Oxford should be ahead on my left. I continued on, pleading with God that the correct airport would appear before me.

And there it was, beyond my left wing, an airport with one runway facing west—Waterbury-Oxford. I dialed in 118.475 and, as if I were totally in control, in my most commanding voice, said, "KOXC tower, this is Piper 55113 coming in to land."

I flew over the trees, then lower, then slower, lower again, nose up, wheels down. And the wheels hit the runway so softly I wondered if I had actually landed. I let out a monster sigh, taxied off the runway and shut down the plane. When I approached the counter of the fixed base operator, I was smiling, and the middle-aged man behind the desk was smiling, too. "Your instructor called me and told me to expect you," he said. "Congratulations!"

I had either misjudged the cross wind or flown too far South leaving Kobelt before turning toward my heading, but, as a result, my path had taken me a few miles off course. I felt as if I had lucked out reaching my destination.

The trip home was easy by comparison; I crossed the Hudson River with Kobalt's one runway glistening right ahead of me and entered the left-hand pattern. Though I landed not quite so softly, my instructor was there to greet me and tell me I had done a good job.

With more experience, I gained confidence and returned to Flight Safety. On a sparkling New Year's day in 1975, I soloed from Vero to Fort Meyers to Palm Beach and back to Vero. Lake Okeechobee stretched out below me, a dazzling deep blue, and, though I was at 5500 feet, the lake seemed so close that I felt I could skim the surface with my fingertips. I rose a thousand feet and watched a pair of gulls below me. They soared sideways with the wind, slid down an air current, then sailed back up. I cut the power and the engine fell silent. The whole world hushed. The Piper and I were flying every bit as gently, as gracefully as the gulls.

In a few minutes I would become just another voice among all the voices clamoring to reach air-traffic control. Soon I'd respond to requests from the tower and fly the rigid landing pattern as precisely as possible with the discipline I'd absorbed during interminable hours of landing drill. But I wasn't ready to land yet. I was still free. I felt perfectly content, as if I were being made love to—slowly, tenderly—in the soft breeze of a summer's afternoon.

Chapter Four

In my 15th year
I asked my mother
if I'd ever be famous.
Why do I still remember
the quick shake
of her head?
If you can answer that,
maybe you
can answer this:
does every mother predict
with an oracle's tongue?

In the early spring of 1975, about a year after I joined *Flying*, Ziff-Davis group vice-president Edward Muhlfeld—pilot, sailor, skier—invited me to join him and his wife and several advertising salesmen and advertisers to ski at Snowmass in Aspen. My first time to schuss in Rocky Mountain powder made for a memorable week. Skiing the Big Burn made me feel more graceful than I had ever been, and moguls were made solely for my idea of twisting, turning—occasionally airborne—fun.

Afterwards, I took some vacation days and went to Denver to meet up with photographer Bruce McAllister, who had garnered an assignment for us from *Colorado* Magazine. Tall and energetic, a Harvard graduate and talented photographer, Bruce had been told as a young man to "go West" and had moved to Denver with an adventurous vengeance. We flew to Wyoming in Bruce's Cessna 182 to interview Clem Skinner, a pioneer trapper and guide who lived in Pinedale near the Wind River Range.

Clem and Vi Skinner had homesteaded there in the 1930's. As a government trapper, he'd captured grizzly bears, wolves and mountain lions. As an outfitter, he'd led long hunting and packing trips into the mountains. His sons now ran a successful wilderness survival camp. But it was a hard interview. Now failing in his health, the old man didn't want to talk about his past. As we sat in his small, close living room, I wondered if I would have a story.

"Tell me about hunting elk," I said.

His face bore an enigmatic smile; he rubbed his scruffy chin. "I'm just an old bear now and not much use to the world anymore."

I kept probing him, but he kept bringing the conversation back to old bears, and, as the afternoon wore on, I gleaned what I could but knew this was going to be a hard story to write. However, I dug into Clem Skinner's history, described the mountains with every adjective I could muster and finally managed to put together a story and sent it off to *Colorado*. As I mailed the story, I wondered if I had written about the real Clem Skinner or invented a hero to fit an image for *Colorado* readers.

♦

As a prestigious magazine, *Flying* was a step up for me. Without a windowed office or the editor's job, it was a step down.

Flying's editor and publisher, Robert Parke, had a devilish management style. He pitted selected co-workers against each other, with the promise of promotion to the winner. Norbert, a brilliant Princeton graduate and my former book editor at Charles Scribner's Sons, now worked across the aisle from me. He puffed on his pipe, spoke in puns and wrote wry copy. He was a Jewish scholar—stocky, a little edgy, wore bifocals—not the hero pilot type, but then, neither was I.

My hair was long, half way down my back, though I sometimes wore it in a French twist. I had begun to color it from medium to dark ash brown to enhance the contrast to my blue eyes. Though hard contact lenses were expensive and difficult to manage in the gritty city streets, I persevered most of the time. For a woman of my generation, at five foot, four inches, I was neither tall nor short. And weighing plus or minus a hundred and fifteen, was neither thin nor fat. In other words, I was overwhelmingly average. A date once commented that I had an English face and a German body. While I didn't appreciate what he said, when I consider those stereotypes, he was probably on to something.

Norbert was my competition for Managing Editor of *Flying*. His forte was grammar and style. I think he knew the *New York Times* stylebook by heart. My strength was enthusiasm, which I felt *Flying* lacked. I fought for it. I sometimes felt that I fought too hard.

About once a week, Parke would give Norb and me the same column or feature to edit overnight. In the morning we were brought in to his office where, his eyebrows rising and falling, mustache twitching, Parke would review and comment upon our work.

Norb was a seasoned book editor. I had ten years of special interest magazine experience, yet I felt that Bob Parke was treating us both like trainees.

On Wednesday, the fourth of June, 1975, after a particularly humiliating session with editor Parke, when he rejected almost all our suggestions on a Richard Collins piece, the whole office disappeared for lunch. I went out to the hallway to buy a sandwich off the cart and settled in at my desk to try to sneak some verve into Collins' latest article on avionics.

Richard Collins knew more about aviation than I would ever know, and would soon become editor of *Flying*. He would log over 20,000 flying hours and produce some eleven respected aeronautical books, yet I was determined to improve this story.

Around 12:30 I received a call from Bruce McAllister. He hesitated on the phone before telling me he had bad news. Clem Skinner, our old bear in Wyoming, had killed his wife then turned the gun on himself.

Bruce would contact the editor at *Colorado* and withdraw the story which they'd accepted for a winter issue.

When he hung up, my stomach churned. I tossed my turkey sandwich into the wastebasket and dropped my head down on my desk.

I had just been in this man's home where I heard him telling me how he felt. Why didn't I realize he was suicidal?

When one of the *Flying* editors came back from lunch, I asked if I could talk to him. He was a young, buttoned-up man with more flying than writing experience. I told him what had happened, and how I felt responsible for telling the truth just as I did whenever I wrote about someone else. What moral right had I to try to define in print someone I hardly knew? It wasn't the first time I'd asked that question

He nodded but looked away. "You're a journalist, right?"

"I guess so," I said. "I always just thought of myself as a writer. But how can I presume to write a profile about someone I've only known for an hour or two? Even for a year or two?"

He stared into a cardboard cup then stirred the coffee. I was beginning to doubt he'd heard what I said. I raised my voice and continued.

"What you see and hear, what you write about, is skewed by what you believe, by what you know. Memory is skewed by intervening events, even by your mood. I don't think there can be true, unbiased writing. Not just about people, but about products as well."

He looked at his watch and shook his head. But I was determined to get a response.

"Think about it. At *Car & Driver,* when we reviewed new cars, we wrote what we thought was true based on our test results, so it was, in a sense, true. But what we wrote was influenced by our exuberance for great cars and for exhilarating automotive experiences. Here, if we don't like something about a new Beech or Cessna, we don't write about it, because the airplane has been tested and approved by the FAA, so there can be nothing wrong with it."

"That's true," he said. "There is no FAA for cars."

His phone rang. "I have to get this," he said and picked up the receiver. He held his hand over the mouthpiece. "Later," he whispered. I left his office feeling both foolish and misunderstood.

I made it through the afternoon, then Norbert and I went out for a drink. I told him about what had happened with Clem Skinner. He sympathized with me. Then we talked about our morning session with Parke.

"It's hopeless," I said. "If it weren't for Richard Bach's occasional stories, Gordon Baxter's column, Peter Garrison's experimental planes, there would be no fun, no romance to the magazine. You and I know flying can be an adventure. It can be exhilarating. It's not all about new gadgets to save the pilot from making his own decisions. I really think I should quit."

He tamped down the tobacco in his pipe, looked at me over the rims of his aviator-shaped glasses and said, "Don't forget that *Amazing Stories* was one of Bill Ziff Senior's first magazines. Maybe we should ask Junior to revive it so we can have some fun." I laughed and went home feeling better.

The next day I heard from *Colorado* magazine. They would not publish the story but would send me a "kill" fee, routinely paid to a contracted freelancer when a story isn't going to run. I told them I didn't want the money. There had been more than enough killing connected to this story. They sent it anyway, and, as it turned out, I would need it.

At the end of the summer I left *Flying* magazine. As I walked from the office with my briefcase and bound copies of magazines which included my stories, I thought I would feel as if I were leaving home. After all, for some ten years, One Park Avenue had been my working home, the place where I spent most of my time alongside other young writers, editors, photographers and artists who were more like adopted siblings than colleagues. But instead, I felt relief.

No more weekly critiques; no more competitions with Norbert, a man whose talent I admired. No more profiles of people I hardly knew. No more betting on the miniscule odds of a woman becoming the editor of another Ziff-Davis magazine anytime in the near future.

Russell Patrick, a friend of mine, was starting a new magazine called *Greenleaves*. I would help him get it off the ground. And I would look for work to provide me with a more promising future.

In fact, I decided to leave publishing altogether to work for an advertising agency where I would be challenged creatively and earn a better salary. Agencies were doing remarkable work, and I could be a part of the exciting trend which began in the '60s with the captivating and honest Doyle Dane Bernbach campaign for Volkswagen: the iconic "Think Small" and "Lemon".

I relished the idea of openly working for clients rather than occasionally battling advertising salesmen whose jobs would be easier if I skewed magazine content to the benefit of our current or potential advertisers.

But to attain a job at an agency would not be easy. As the saying went, to work on a white bread account, you needed white bread experience. I had no white bread, brown bread, no advertising experience at all. I spent the fall of 1975 looking for the right job.

I called in every debt owed me by friends, asking for leads and references. I sent out resumes and pounded the streets, and the streets pounded me. The slushy day I was due at J. Walter Thompson, a yellow cab raced by and sprayed my white wool interview suit with wet sludge, and I began to wonder whether jail wouldn't be a better alternative. I would, at least, be fed and housed, and my orange prison jumpsuit wouldn't need dry cleaning.

I dismissed the thought, went uptown to Vidal Sassoon and asked for the top stylist to cut my long hair into a bouncing, geometric bob. I charged it on my credit card and danced out of the salon, swinging my head past every mirror.

And wondrously, just a week later, I landed a good job at Dancer-Fitzgerald-Sample, one of Manhattan's best advertising agencies at the time—the thirteenth largest in the world.

I was ecstatic. I could put my imaginative powers to work and pay my credit card bill. My job combined both account and creative work for special promotional campaigns. I'd be assigned Toyota, Duracell, Arby's, and work with others in the department on Hamm's Beer, Hanes, including L'eggs, Proctor & Gamble, Reynolds and General Mills. That night I called my mother with the good news.

"But honey," she said. "You don't like to type."

"You don't need to worry about it, Mom. I think that's what my secretary is supposed to do."

Chapter Five

Dad,
because you were
who you were: handsome, hero
of a realm
beyond the stuff
of children's imaginings
is it any wonder
we thought you knew
what you were doing to us—
and why?

My father was intelligent, forthright, a hero, strikingly handsome with black hair, prominent cheekbones and dark eyes, though, like all men, he possessed inconsistencies. In photographs, the right side of his face often appears to be reaching out to embrace the world, the left side retreating.

Before the USA entered World War II, my father, a Major in the Army Corps of Engineers, was in charge of designing and constructing four air bases near San Antonio, Texas. Right after Pearl Harbor was bombed (and six months before I was born), he shipped out to Honolulu. He was promoted to Colonel and became District Engineer in charge of building air bases, seacoast artillery installations, harbors, batteries, housing and service facilities in preparation for the Pacific Theater assault on Japan. Before the year was over, he became commander of construction in the Central Pacific area, in charge of some 15,000 Engineer troops and 20,000 civilians.

As the fighting moved closer to Tokyo, so did my father. For five months, from April to August, 1945, under combat conditions, he was responsible for designing and constructing the airbase and support facilities on Iejima, an island within hollering distance of Okinawa. The month before he arrived, the Japanese had destroyed the Iejima runways, believing—correctly—that the island would fall to the Allies. After Japanese planes bombed the airfield, their foot soldiers crisscrossed the island to bury unused aerial bombs and explosives made from drums of gasoline.

It took my father, with the troops he commanded, less than a month to dismantle the mines and ready the three runways and accompanying taxiways for operations. Iejima became home to the 413th Fighter Group and the 345th Bombardment Group, a strategic base to support operations against Okinawa and, later, against the Japanese homeland.

The battle of Okinawa began that April and lasted for eighty-two days. Fighting was ferocious, with intense kamikaze attacks from the Japanese, and the allies suffered 65,000 casualties. On April 18, 1945, legendary journalist

Ernie Pyle was one of the casualties. He was gunned down by a sniper on Iejima.

Before my father left Iejima in August, 1945, two Japanese Mitsubishi G4M Betty bombers flew into the airfield under B-25 escort. Japanese dignitaries emerged from the Bettys and were transferred to US Army Air Force C-54's headed for the Philippines. When they arrived in Manila, they concluded arrangements for the September 2nd formal surrender to General McArthur's staff. My father would receive a Legion of Merit medal for his outstanding accomplishments in Hawaii and on Iejima.

During a month of leave after the surrender, Dad returned to San Antonio and finally met me. I was three years old.

Next he was ordered to Japan as a commander under the Eighth Army to rebuild and reconstruct air bases in Japan and Korea. In the fall of 1945 my mother, brother and sister and I boarded a troop ship for Japan to live at Yokota air base, originally an Imperial Japanese Army flight test center.

None of us knew at that time that Dad had fallen in love with Esther Smith, a civilian secretary he had met in Hawaii, and that year in Japan was the only time he and I would reside in the same house. My parents were in the process of a divorce when he shipped back to Atlanta to head the South Atlantic Division of the Corps of Engineers. We followed him to Atlanta, but Esther arrived sooner.

I seldom saw him since his career took my father and Esther from Atlanta to the Pentagon, then Turkey, Greece, France, back to Hawaii then to Italy until, in the mid-1960s, they retired in rural Mathews County in Virginia's Tidewater region.

My father was a fantasy figure—and at times the aching hollow just below my sternum. All I knew about him was what I was told, and I was told very little, yet when I gazed at his picture beside my bed, I knew he was more handsome than any of my friends' fathers, and none of them were Colonels, so he must have been more important, too. My father was the first of my loves to disappear into the ether like an azure balloon.

After I began working in New York, I found the courage to visit my father and Esther in Mathews, Virginia. I returned from time to time and began to feel a little more comfortable with both of them. They had no children together, and neither my brother nor my sister had seen him in several years. For more than twenty years, his role as a father seemed limited to a birthday message seldom longer than "love, Dad". I was surprised and pleased that he now appeared to look forward to my visits, and I felt fortunate to have reconnected with him.

Once robust, a cadet captain and football player at West Point, class of '29, by the 1970s, Dad had grown thin to the point of appearing frail, though he still worked in his shop and garden, and his arm muscles bulged when he swung a mallet. With his face now thinner, his cheekbones appeared more prominent, and his brown eyes were magnified by thick lenses after cataract surgery, the only option in the days before implants. A stroke had restricted his swallowing. My handsome hero was aging awkwardly.

I began to see my father more regularly—at least a couple of times a year—and as I think back, I understand that, while I may have thought I was finally securing for myself the father I had wanted as a child, I may also have been giving him back one of his three children, a gift that might have meant more to him than I was able to understand at the time.

♦

While I want to gather the threads of my mother's life to make a whole quilt, many essential squares are missing. Like most of us today, she was a woman who lived in complex times and was forced to deal with unrehearsed problems.

My mother, Honora, grew up a privileged child of older parents, and was their only child until a sister was adopted.

Her mother, my grandmother, was one of ten children, born on a remote farm near Broadclyst, Devon, England, and, with one of her sisters, immigrated to the United States to study nursing. She obtained her degree in Indianapolis in 1897. My grandfather, Jay Lott Warren, the son of a jeweler, was a businessman who worked with emerging enterprises—predominantly oil companies—in the western states. They were married at Ascension Parish on the corner of

Fifth Avenue and Tenth Street, New York, on the seventh of May, 1903.

Mother was born in March, 1910, in Colorado Springs, when her parents were in their mid-thirties. Shortly thereafter, the Warren family moved into a large home at 890 Logan Street in Denver. Although, in 1958, the house was torn down and an apartment building erected on the lot, the state governor continues to occupy the mansion across the street.

My grandfather also owned some grazing land in Kansas and a 1200-acre working ranch near Castle Rock, Colorado. After he died in July, 1937, my grandmother sold at auction the ranch, including seventeen head of cattle, one bull, eight horses, plows, cultivators, binders, wagons, mowers, dairy equipment, tractors and a 1928 Ford truck. She kept the 1934 seven-passenger Cadillac sedan.

Mother attended East Denver High and, for a semester, National Cathedral School in Washington, DC. After a tour of Europe where she was enchanted by her handsome British cousins, and a year at Colorado College, she attended Denver University and met my father who was stationed at Fort Logan, a former frontier fort turned military base on the outskirts of Denver. Like my grandparents, they were married on the seventh of May. The year was 1931, six months after their engagement was announced.

Mother was, no doubt, smitten by the handsome and intelligent young first lieutenant who had recently graduated from the U.S. Military

Academy. From a civil servant family in Indiana, he may have been awed by the Warren family.

I have always doubted that my mother was fully prepared to endure life on army posts with the pecking-order protocol and long separations in times of war.

When my parents divorced in 1947, my grandmother made the down payment on a house in Atlanta. My mother was working, first in a doctor's office, then as a school secretary, and finally as a registrar where she traveled extensively to recruit students for The Piedmont Hospital School of Nursing.

My grandmother lived with us until she died in September, 1952, when I was ten years old. Because my mother worked full time, losing my grandmother was like losing my closest parent. It was she who looked after me, cleaned me up after school for piano lessons and ballet classes, cooked our meals and performed as a patient opponent in endless games of checkers. The trust fund she left my mother was to pay for her grandchildren's education.

I was too young at the time to wonder how lonely my grandmother must have been, a widow, cut off from all of her British family. She was hard of hearing, walked with a cane and no longer drove. She wrote copious numbers of letters to the UK, and there were weekly letters in our mailbox with blue, green, red or brown stamps picturing George VI.

My mother was a divorcee and single mother several decades before the term "single parent" was generally used. Her status was abnormal enough to appear to be an embarrassment to her. Some two years after my parents separated, an au pair looking after the children who lived down the street spitefully told me that my parents were divorced. When I returned home in tears and confronted my mother, she finally told me it was true, and that Daddy wouldn't be living with us again. I cried for hours, feeling not only forsaken but betrayed.

In the predominately Jewish middle-class neighborhood where I lived during my primary school years, I remember only one other single-parent household, and that parent was a father. Yet, by 2012, nearly a third of all households were maintained by a single parent, quadrupling the number in the late 1940s.

I doubt that the some twenty-one million children now living apart from one of their parents finds growing up any easier than we did. While today's children of single parents may be more readily accepted by the community at large and have more friends also shaped by divorce, they still return to a home which has been riven; where implicit anxiety and despondency may more freely creep from room to room than in healthy two-parent households.

My mother employed three prominent traits to great advantage. First, she abided by the social protocol of her tea-dance upbringing and expected the same of others. On the other hand, she was adventurous and prone to do as she chose. She would plan elaborate trips to travel with her children across the country or to visit cousins in England.

She also readily summoned others for help, for advice and for affection. If what she desired was not forthcoming, tears accompanied by wide-eyed pleading sometimes worked. The help she accepted; the advice she generally ignored; the love never seemed quite sufficient.

♦

In March of 1976, my stepmother, Esther, was undergoing a procedure to insert a pacemaker. Just before noon Dad called me at the office. "She didn't survive the operation," he said, and, for the first time in my life, I heard him cry. I cleared my desk, ran home and packed and, that afternoon, was on my way to LaGuardia to fly to Virginia.

I was uneasy; I wondered if I could give Dad the support he surely needed. After all these years I had still not made peace with my stepmother. Since my mother blamed Esther for stealing our father away from us, I'd dealt with Esther as if through a glass windowpane. I'd be in the same room with her, respectful but distant enough to avoid feeling disloyal to my mother. I hadn't even told my mother that Esther had died, not wanting her to know where I was.

We left Dad's house in Mathews and drove out past the small town of Hudgins, then turned down a gravel lane toward the cemetery. I breathed deeply and beseeched courage, just as I had when I entered the funeral parlor where PK's family insisted he be laid out, rouged and waxy like an effigy bearing no likeness to the man I wanted to remember.

At least there would not be a body this time. I wouldn't have to look down on Esther with her short now-gray hair, softly delineated face, rounded nose, so different from my mother whose hair grew blonder and nose thinner, more aristocratic, each passing year.

Beyond a few dozen headstones was a cove, looking somewhat dreary under a covering of March clouds. We walked slowly toward the bay, toward the breakwater, where a small group of people had gathered. Dad took my hand and held onto it.

During the service Dad stood, as if in a trance, looking out over the water. It wasn't until the minister scattered a handful of dirt across the urn lying in a small, square pit, and began to intone "dust to dust," that Dad removed his hand from mine and finally looked down at the burial site. When he looked up again, he searched the crowd and seemed not only forlorn, but lost, even bewildered.

I followed his gaze then looked down and noticed the stone next to Esther's gravesite:

A child, a baby, lay in the grave beside her. This was not Esther's child, but none the less a child who was born and also died in 1964. I wondered if this baby had been stillborn; I hoped she had lived long enough to feel a mother's, a father's arms around her.

When the service was over, Dad stood silently beside Esther's grave for a long while, then finally took my hand once more and let me lead him toward the car. He turned once and looked back toward the bay. When his eyes rested on the gravesite, he said, "She is such a lady. Such a fine lady."

"I'm sorry, Dad," I said. "This is very painful for you."

He swallowed hard. I searched for the words that meant the most to me when PK died.

"She loved you, Dad. She was...."

Before I could continue, he interrupted me: "No, Kid. Not was. Esther is. She is, damn it. She still is."

I understood completely. For all of the complexities which brought us together and apart, PK, also, still was.

As we approached his car, Esther's good friend Phoebe Stiles waited while other friends and neighbors offered Dad their condolences. When she came forward she hugged Dad, wiped a tear from his cheek and told him that she would be watching out for him. Then she hugged me.

"Esther often talked about you," she said. "She so wanted a daughter."

But I had been a reluctant daughter to Esther. She had welcomed me into her home with a kind, if shy, encouragement. I wondered if I had not judged her wrongly, basing my detachment on my mother's feelings rather than being open to my own sentiments. It troubled me greatly that I might have allowed my mother to influence my relationship with Esther, and now I had no way of repairing the wrong I might have done.

♦

I liked Phoebe Stiles from the start. She was astute and observant, a quiet woman, solid both in stature and outlook. It didn't take me long to realize that she was the ship's mast for her two sons and her husband's often free-flying sails.

Hamilton (Tony) Stiles, a handsome, gregarious man with a nearly full head of silver hair, could perform any music by ear. He'd played brass instruments in a band before joining the Merchant Marines in World War II. Then, despite the lack of a college education, he became a successful broker in the paper business, making a small fortune with the invention of the cardboard tube for the tampon. He enjoyed his toys, especially the sailboats he bought then learned to sail on the New England coast. And he loved his boys, Hamilton William Stiles, Jr., an aircraft engineer who had graduated from MIT, and David Daggett Stiles, a Dartmouth College English major with graduate work in beef cattle husbandry at Oregon State who then followed his father into the paper business.

Often acting the part of a carefree rascal, Tony laughed at himself in a stand-up New York accent. But he was self-confident, proud of his achievements and generous with his dry martinis. He retired in his early forties to Oakland Farm in Mathews, Virginia, 196 acres with frontage where the Blackwater and Oakland Creeks flow into the North River. He raised and bred Black Angus cattle, kept a mule, and later, pigs.

The day after Esther's funeral, Tony asked Dad to come over to help him with an electrical problem on his Grand Banks trawler. I was invited to tag along.

Dad went into his workshop and came out with one of his several electric meters and a red tool box. "Tony is always having some kind of problem. Doesn't know a damn thing about how to fix anything." His smile was proud, but his broad lower lip pouted slightly.

We turned off North River Road and drove down the long tree-lined lane, passing neatly plowed fields and a barn before we arrived at the large, stately white house on the river, its entrance flanked by four tall Doric columns. Out front was a beautifully-restored 1931 Model A Ford Coupe. Dad went to the door of the house while I walked around the car, admiring the rumble seat, skinny white-walled tires and bright-red hubs.

Phoebe came to the door and called out to me: "I see you have met Tony's girlfriend, Annabelle!" I laughed and walked toward the door. She turned to call inside: "Tony! Ben and Sally are here!"

Oakland Farm was far more impressive than my father's home, but I felt comfortable as soon as I walked in. While many of my friends' parents had grand houses, the rooms sometimes seemed as contrived as the pictures in *House Beautiful*, designed to be envied rather than enjoyed. Both the antique furnishings and the owners of

59

Oakland Farm were without pretense and made me feel welcome.

I admired the pool table in the billiards room, and Tony offered to stand me to a game of eight-ball while Dad and Phoebe talked. Tony's pool cue was a handsome stick, studded with mother of pearl. Though he appeared to approach his shots nonchalantly, his fingers were large and strong, and his aim was deadly.

Once he miscued and laughed off his error. He seemed to be having a good time, and I suspected it didn't take much to amuse him; he'd prefer to laugh than to contemplate sad or disturbing thoughts.

I still had three striped balls on the table when he sunk the last solid, then hesitated for only a second, pretended to look perplexed, pointed his stick at the far corner pocket, and caromed the cue ball off a spot just left of the middle pocket. The cue ball solidly struck the eight ball, which rolled into the corner, hesitated on the edge, then disappeared into the pocket.

He put his arm around my shoulder as we walked to the screened porch where Dad and Phoebe were talking. "You're not too bad for a girl," he said. He was teasing me in a gentle way. I was captivated and smiled at him, then suggested a rematch on my next visit.

Dad followed Tony down to the dock, and Phoebe and I sat in comfortable wicker chairs on the porch; she poured iced tea then lit a thin, dark brown cigarette and took a puff. She carefully put the cigarette down in the ashtray beside her. Her eyes formed engaging half moons, and her mouth opened slightly into a contented smile. "We have a son, David. He is in Algeria, managing operations for a paper mill." Her smile disappeared. "He's divorced. It was—"

She paused and shook her head. "It was hard on him. . . especially because . . ." Again she paused, looked down and dropped her hands to her lap. She swallowed then spoke again:

"Because of the children."

I nodded, wondering what was to follow. Her cigarette exuded a thin whiff of smoke which drifted between us before dying out.

Then she spoke more rapidly. "His home office is in New York, and he is there from time to time. Would it be okay if . . . if I gave him your phone number?"

Phoebe picked up her glass and once again paused. She put the glass down without taking a sip.

"Of course," I said. If David were anything like his father, that was more than okay with me.

By the time Dad and Tony reappeared, both Phoebe and I were smiling.

♦

In the evening over cocktails on Dad's porch overlooking Put-In-Creek, I told my father what Phoebe said. He shifted in his chair, took a long swallow of Old Forester, closed his eyes, as he sometimes did when he was thinking. Then he opened his eyes and said, "Of the two, Bill, the older boy, is the better choice. He's steady,

consistent, like Phoebe. Of course he's married."
His lower lip spread into that little pout.

"David takes after Tony. And you never know what Tony's up to."

I didn't like what he was saying, but I was used to Dad being critical.

"Another thing," Dad said. "David and his ex-wife married while he was still in college; they have a passel of kids—I think there are five of them."

Five children seemed more of a bonus than a detriment to me. I had gone too long with none of my own.

Dad summed up his feelings. "I'm not saying you shouldn't see him, Kiddo, but I'm telling you like it is."

At that moment, I couldn't have been happier to have finally found a father who cared about me enough to give advice. At the same time, despite his reservations about David, I couldn't have been more pleased that I might one day meet an eligible son of two people I liked enormously: Tony and Phoebe Stiles.

Chapter Six

Beneath the ripples
in this reflection pond
lies an old penny
somewhat imagined,
somewhat dreamed—
the date a little fuzzy, the face
a little blurred—
I have a choice:

I leave the penny; let the years
scuff off the truth
or expose it to
this morning's sun,
turn it this way and that,
burnish it to
a newly-minted dazzle.

On the thirteenth of July, 1976, the corn growing in pots in my New York apartment had reached two and a half feet, overshadowed only by four spindly trees sprouted from avocado seeds. The tomato plant was too small to need staking.

The wind rose, gusting through the apartment, and as I shut the window to save the corn stalks from toppling off the radiator, I heard a crash in the bedroom. The curtain was flapping across my bedside table, and PK's photograph was on the floor, upside down, the glass in the frame broken into dozens of splinters.

PK had died exactly two years before, and I'd thought about him all day. His spirit obviously responded to my emotions and flew in for a visit, but left—quickly—the same way he entered, through my ninth floor bedroom window. I stuck my head out the window to watch the traffic parade slowly down Park Avenue. Not a single leaf stirred among the Ash trees below me.

The photograph on the floor was of PK walking through the woods with a friend's child by his side. He wore a black cashmere turtleneck and smiled his loopy grin. His large black eyes were hidden by sunglasses. I started to reach down to smooth a wide, thick sideburn, and noticed a deep gash across the lower right hand side of the picture. I withdrew my hand, picked up the picture and carefully placed it upside down in the dustpan, then swept up the glass.

Next to the window was a whalebone mask I had bought in Skagway, Alaska, during my snowmobiling expedition to the Chilkoot. I thought it would be a beneficial spirit, a talisman to uplift my soul, but that night the lifeless eyes, the carved smile on its rough face turned bitter. I removed the mask from the nail.

I went down the hall to the incinerator with both the dustpan and the mask. I listened while glass and bone tumbled down ten stories to the basement and knew that something very sad though, at the same time, redemptive, had just occurred.

♦

A therapist was helping me sort out my relationship with PK and its aftermath. He was a behaviorist and was using relaxation response technique, a form of directed meditation, which eliminated my occasional bouts of anxiety.

But when I complained to him about the high cost of his weekly services, he suggested I give up my apartment and rent a cheap room in Queens. Was he nuts? I had a superb rent-stabilized apartment with windows overlooking both Park Avenue and 35th street.

A paraplegic photo re-toucher lived in the penthouse. An intensely Jewish hypnotist lived next door. At the end of my hall was a husky Swedish blonde recently divorced from a TV weatherman, and next to her a very proper matron who often wore a veiled hat. Lou, an attractive, vivacious personal-injury lawyer rented a studio downstairs. A few floors above me lived a flight attendant who served those who flew on cargo planes. Next door to her was an elegant, kind and unconventional woman, an executive assistant for the hottest ad agency in town. Her husband lived in Maryland and collected 5-cent return bottles whenever he came to New York.

The building was a block away from my former office at Ziff-Davis and now ten blocks from my office on Madison Avenue. Downhill and half a block away on Lexington Avenue was the Guardsman, a pub with an appropriate smoky, stale-beer tavern smell. They served excellent sandwiches, especially the reasonably-priced egg salad, onion and bacon stuffed into pita bread. There were backgammon tables and a prominent dart board. Usually there was a liar's dice game in progress. It was a perfect place to hang out with neighborhood friends on nights when I was in town and didn't have anything special to do.

After I disposed of the picture and the mask, the Swede knocked on my door and invited me to join her at the Guardsman. While we ate, she talked about her ex-husband, nothing I hadn't heard before. I talked about Al One and Al Two, the men I was regularly dating, nothing she hadn't heard before. Al One was a querulous Jewish psychotherapist; the other Al worked on Wall Street, and his parents owned a Fifth Avenue penthouse. The French Impressionist paintings in the living room had been chosen by a decorator. I was not impressed.

But I was thinking about something else entirely—something my analyst had said. "You know, Sally, you gave PK what could have been the best years of your life." During those ten years most of my friends had found spouses and become mothers to inquisitive, funny children who drew stick pictures and signed them "I love you, Mommy."

Perhaps I was lucky to have been able to find my own way in a rewarding career; to have a number of friends I could trust to care about me, as I cared about them. Or maybe I had simply dribbled away my life on frivolous jobs and a man who was unable or unwilling to envision a more significant future together. Had we married, maybe I would have been forced to take unwelcome detours or to dwell unhappily in stifling hollows for long periods of time. Perhaps or perhaps not. I would never know.

For the first time, I accepted the "perhaps" along with the "perhaps not". I felt grateful for the years of experience, of growth as a human being navigating young adulthood in New York City.

When I walked home from the Guardsman that night I felt as if half a dozen heavy wet coats were slipping from my shoulders, one by one. I was ready for a peaceful, dreamless sleep. It may have been the Jack Daniel's. It may have been because I let the photo go. It may even have been because I destroyed the mask. It was probably because I could finally acknowledge it had been my choice to give those years to PK. I, alone, was responsible for my decisions. And I had gained as well as lost.

Nine days earlier, on Sunday, July Fourth, a Bicentennial tall ship sailed proudly into New York harbor; composer Leonard Bernstein conducted a rousing concert in Central Park and fireworks dazzled Sheep Meadow. Just the night before, I sat transfixed before my small black and white TV as civil rights leader and member of the House of Representatives Barbara Jordan delivered her electrifying keynote speech to the Democratic convention, the first ever by a black woman. "As a first step," she said, "we must restore belief in ourselves . . . . A nation is formed by the willingness of each of us to share in the responsibility for upholding the common good."

These were exciting times for my country and for me. I wanted to be as inspiring as Leonard Bernstein; as smart and eloquent as Barbara Jordan. While I had never colored inside the lines, I realized I could ignore the lines completely and draw new pictures of my own imagining. After all, had I not been given a life of my own that begged to be lived uniquely?

I would be authentic. An existentialist might take that to mean being true to one's own spirit rather than conforming to imposed values. But, more easily, I embraced Eric Fromm's notion that if I seriously considered the implications of prevailing social norms, I might accept some of them and reject others. I could work hard to convince women to buy L'eggs pantyhose, a product which freed them of garters, but could refuse to work on Count Chocula cereal with all those marshmallows, more sugar than nutrition—and pitched exclusively to children.

The personal philosophy I was accepting gave me many opportunities for rationalization, but most importantly it urged me to make the most of the rest of my life and to fully accept responsibility for my decisions and to lay aside blame.

I would ditch Al One and Al Two. Perhaps I would continue to solo from adventure to adventure. Or perhaps—just perhaps—like Sir Henry Stanley found Doctor David Livingstone, I would stumble upon a man with whom I would share the rest of my journey.

He and I would have long-ago cast off our chains, worn out and discarded our disguises. Sunlight would follow us through the landscape of possibility. And a beautiful azure balloon would hover between the two of us, never desiring to fly away. Perhaps or perhaps not.

That night the calendar flipped over. The next morning, the fourteenth of July, it felt like New Year's Day.

In the coming months a New York buccaneer bought my apartment building, and I led the tenants into battle. I was sent to Tucson to work on the L'eggs tennis tournament and then to California to work with our client, Toyota. My story on racecar driver Bobby Allison was reprinted in a fifty-year commemorative book, *The Best of Flying*.

In addition, Helen Gurley Brown had agreed to buy a story on learning to fly which I'd proposed for *Cosmopolitan*, and *Americana* was interested in an article about antique cameras. Occasionally, I still flew small planes, and, once again, felt the elation of gaining altitude off a runway and leisurely exploring the vast skies above me, the earth in miniature below.

I'd jotted down a number from a subway ad asking for volunteers and became a tutor to Timmy, a young Puerto Rican who had dropped out of high school and was struggling to obtain his GED. I helped him improve his reading level from grade four to grade eight, and the more I worked with him, the more I wanted him to succeed. I had been given so many advantages, and Timmy had received so few. Although he was unremarkable in appearance, rather scrawny, and spoke in a timid lisp, when the spark concealed within him was ignited, his dark eyes flashed with excitement, he responded with assurance, and I knew there was a chance he would succeed.

And I would succeed as well. I had not experienced an anxiety attack in months. I had a good job at a great agency and would develop my talents even further; if I worked hard enough and the fates were with me, I could become a vice-president before I turned thirty-five.

Chapter Seven

For all we know
there is so much more
we can only wish
we knew,
and
what we know about what
we know
is nothing.

It was a sweltering Friday in August, 1976, just after noon and a little over a month since PK's apparition flashed through my apartment. I was alone in my office as the rest of the staff had left for the day. Casual Fridays and Friday afternoons off in the summer were our reward for coming in early the rest of the week.

David Stiles was to appear at any moment, so I was having trouble concentrating on the report about the college market I was writing for Toyota. I heard his footsteps in the hall, then a handsome head peered around the corner of my office door. Handsome but. . . uh, oh.

His hair was not thick and ample like his father's. In fact, there was only a suggestion of hair swept back from his forehead beside a carefully-combed part.

He smiled warmly, his brown eyes sparkled, and he said: "Wow!"

I watched his eyes sweep my fairly spacious, colorfully-decorated office, including for a brief moment the woman his mother had urged him to call.

Tall, slender, well over six feet, his legs were long, stomach flat. Tufts of dark reddish chest hair rose behind his open-collared, button-down yellow Oxford shirt. He was wearing a summer-weight maroon sport jacket.

He chose a very nice upscale French restaurant off Third Avenue. As typical, there were tables for two along the walls, and centered above each was a painting reminiscent of the work of a Montmartre street artist. In the middle were tables for four with just enough space between them for the sommelier to weave in and out and the bus boy to move with a tray held well above his head. There were a few other patrons in the restaurant, but not enough to make it too loud to talk or too stifling to be comfortable. It felt as if we were alone.

David ordered a Bloody Mary. I chose a glass of Dubonnet. He told me a little bit about his job. He was working for Parsons and Whittemore, a private company owned by the Landegger family. The firm was one of the world's largest market pulp producers and also ran turnkey engineering and construction projects for pulp and paper mills world-wide.

He talked about the paper mill in Mostaganem, a port city founded in the 11th century in Northwestern Algeria on the Alboran Sea. He told me about the beaches, to which Algerians teemed each summer, and about

Tidgit, the ancient Muslim sector across the wadi, the Moorish architecture of the buildings, and the minarets scattered throughout the city, the amplified sound of the muezzin calling the faithful to adhān.

He nodded toward the kitchen. "When I go into the market, the chickens are caged. Alive. Or hanging by their necks. At first, the smell was overpowering, and I just wanted to walk away, but I knew I had to eat, so I learned to pick out the fattest chickens and bring them home. And then I figured out how to gut them."

He laughed. "At least the lettuce and green vegetables are fresh and quite nice," he said. "Once you've picked out the worms."

He leaned across the table, his mouth forming a gentle but knowing smile. "You should have seen the kitchen after I cut up that first bird. The whole place looked like an abattoir."

I flinched. "I can't imagine. . .everything I buy at the supermarket. . . ." Then I laughed. "Actually, most of what I buy doesn't require a lot of cooking. I don't have much of a kitchen."

Then he lowered his head and looked at me with concern. "But why am I talking about this? We're about to have lunch."

The waiter appeared. David ordered steamed mussels. I ordered escargot and, despite his previous description of Algerian greens, a salad.

As we ate, I noticed how deftly he controlled his knife and fork. My father had told me that David had fallen from a tree when he was eight years old; the cast was wound too tight, and, as a result, he had almost lost his left arm to gangrene. As a child he endured numerous surgeries to restore movement to his arm and structure to his hand. Before I met him, I wondered how much impairment he suffered. While he had little use of his left hand, it didn't seem to bother him. He used both hands, the right for precise tasks and the left as he could. I was impressed by how he seemed to accept himself as he was without self-consciousness.

He asked me about my job, and we talked about the advertising world, and then about our parents. He told me he felt secure in his relationship with his father and mother. "They have become like a cashmere scarf which feels comfortable around my neck," he said.

"Wow!" I said. "That's a beautiful description. I envy that." I told him how much I liked them, and about the game of eight-ball I lost to his dad. He cocked his head and squinted down at me. "Hmmn. Dad must have been practicing. He didn't used to be that good."

I laughed. "He seemed pretty skillful to me. My British managing editor, Caroline, and I learned to shoot pool from a hustler at a pool hall on Broadway. But I'm out of practice, not that I was ever very good."

I asked him questions about Algeria, a nation of Berbers who had been exploited by Spain, the Ottoman Empire, the Holy Roman Empire, Barbary Pirates and France. Most of what I knew about the country—and it wasn't much—came from having read Albert Camus' *The Stranger* at least four times.

"Is it terribly hot, and does the beach pulse with the heat, like Camus describes?"

"Yes." He nodded. "It can be insufferably hot. But there was a rare Sirocco a few weeks ago. The Sahara winds moved north, and around three in the morning the temperature rose to 100 degrees and stayed there for five days. I knew I was being cooked, but no perspiration was visible. Zero humidity."

"What about the language?" I asked. "How do you communicate?"

"The majority of workers in the mill speak Arabic or French," he said. "I only took Spanish in school. I use pidgin, gestures, sometimes translators. And I'm picking up quite a bit of French."

He paused and lit a Benson & Hedges from a foreign pack, took a slow puff before continuing. "Though they have little experience with papermaking, the workers are learning, and I feel good about that. His eyes lit up and I felt drawn into his face, into his smile which enticed small crinkles to appear on either side of his eyes. He was animated, aware and articulate.

He took another puff, put the cigarette down in the ashtray and picked up his water glass. His right hand fingers were long and looked strong, pleasingly masculine. He took a sip, put the glass down, picked up the cigarette, blew a stream of smoke into the aisle and continued:

"I know this Frenchman from another project," he said. "Most of us are paid in U.S. dollars deposited at home, but we need walk-around cash for day-to-day expenses. So this guy

75

hides cash between slabs of bacon. The Muslim customs inspectors won't touch the pork." He chuckled.

I sat back in my chair, perturbed at what I was hearing.

"And you think that's okay?" My face must have shown my discomfort.

He gave me a questioning look, seemed puzzled, put out his cigarette. He cleared his throat but didn't answer.

From that point onward, I heard nothing he was really saying. What I imagined was the cynical arrogance of so many young men I'd known over the past ten years who boasted about side-stepping the military system in Vietnam; who often ridiculed both the Vietnamese they were defending and those they were fighting. I also heard my father's warnings.

At that moment I assumed we had nothing in common, and wondered why this well-educated and obviously intelligent man was wringing chicken necks in Algeria instead of pursuing a meaningful career in New York. In fact, I understood nothing at all about North Africa and less about him.

A few sentences had killed my interest, my short-lived fantasy that this spirited, charming man might become important to me. On reflection, as the meal was ending, I might have been looking for an excuse to dislike him. I wasn't ready to become involved with another man who was about to leave me.

After lunch, I headed out to my shared summer house in the Hamptons. He left to visit his brother in Port Jefferson and would fly back to Mostaganem before I returned to the city on Monday morning. I doubted I would ever see him again.

Chapter Eight

And the city
whispered to me:
within my vast cloaks
are hidden many keys—
some filigreed, some dense—
one unchains compassion,
and one the teeming labyrinth
of hope.

One leads back
to beginnings, and one
to distant encounters.
One unlocks
the gate to love;
one unlocks
mere chattel.

In 1977, much was rotten in the Big Apple. In fact, many felt it was rotten to the core. Since its after-war glory days of the 1950s, industry had abandoned Manhattan for cheaper and easier places to operate, and the white flight to the suburbs left the city with a huge welfare burden.

A nine-day garbage strike in 1968 was only the beginning of what would become a stinking mess.

During the seventies, the question was when—not if—the city would default on its loans and declare bankruptcy. In 1975, when Gerald Ford refused a bailout to the city, the *New York Daily News* issued its famous headline which summarized what a lot of people felt about New York: "Ford to City: Drop Dead."

The subway system was better known as a gallery for graffiti than for reliable and safe transportation. Central Park became a place to go if you were looking for a mugger, and drug dealers were the unelected governors of all the smaller pocket parks. There were more prostitutes and pimps in Times Square than there were aspiring actors. Fire stations were shut down and policemen laid off.

Two years before, terrorism struck when FALN, the armed forces of the Puerto Rican National Liberation, blew up Fraunces Tavern, the historic restaurant on Pearl Street where George Washington said farewell to his Revolutionary War officers.

By 1977, David Berkowitz, The Son of Sam, a serial killer, was roaming the streets, shooting young dark-haired women with his .44 Bulldog revolver. He was also sending hand-written letters to *Daily News* columnist Jimmy Breslin and NYPD Captain Joseph Borelli.

Berkowitz didn't think much of New York either. A letter to Breslin began: "Hello from the gutters of N.Y.C. which are filled with dog manure, vomit, stale wine, urine and blood. . . ."

However, all that being said, New York was still the place to be in the United States if you wanted to establish yourself in publishing, advertising, finance, fashion, art, music or the stage. In Manhattan you could meet and mingle with some of the most creative, interesting (and some of the most delightfully bizarre) people in the world. And the mid-seventies was a time of intense creativity.

Artists had begun moving into SoHo and renovating neglected lofts. Broadway was afire with notable productions, and one could buy a Standing Room Only ticket for a few dollars to watch such greats as *Tiny Alice, The Cherry Orchard, Oliver, Hello Dolly, The Prime of Miss Jean Brodie, Fiddler on the Roof, Godspell, Annie, The Crucible, Oh, Calcutta, Funny Girl, A Doll's House, Hair, The Three Penny Opera, Jesus Christ Superstar, Grease, Man of La Mancha, Mame.* Afterwards, for the price of a drink, you could slip into Sardi's to mingle with or goggle at members of the cast. I even acted as a supernumerary when Gian-Carlo Menotti directed *The Saint of Bleeker Street* at Lincoln Center. Jackie Kennedy came to the dress rehearsal. Heady stuff.

While I had been to every state in the USA and most of the provinces in Canada, and often found myself in a bucolic mountain or ocean village yearning for a more tranquil life; while I still wanted to grow my own vegetables, even if unsuccessfully in a city apartment, I was proud of being a New Yorker with an interesting job and an apartment in Murray Hill. New York seemed to me to be smarter, classier than cities in the Midwest, more of an amalgam of the world, more serious than those in California, and much less restrictive, less intolerant than cities in the South.

With full days at the office and a good deal of work-related travel, it always felt good to come back home. My living room was just big enough for a white leather hide-a-bed sofa and an antique porcelain barber chair I had brought from my office at Ziff-Davis. The big, reclining chair had cost $25 when the barber off the lobby went out of business. My coffee table was a three-foot round of plywood squatting on a truck tire scavenged from Little West 12th Street.

The longest wall was lined with books. I still had some of my college textbooks, primarily philosophy books and anthologies of plays. I had recently studied with Lee Minoff, who wrote the screenplay for the Beetles' *Yellow Submarine* and began to fancy myself a budding screenwriter. The nonsensical (and much for that reason) meaningful work of absurdist playwrights like Edward Albee and Samuel Beckett fascinated me.

A lapsed Episcopalian, still arrogant enough to attempt to create a God who made sense, I plowed through Christian philosophers such as C. S. Lewis and Paul Tillich. Also, I was adding to a library of contemporary psychology.

Charles Scribner's Sons was my favorite bookstore, and not just because they had published my only book to date. Walking through the glass and brass doors at 597 Fifth Avenue felt like entering a sanctuary which housed significant information about things that mattered in the world. I revered the famous Scribner's editor, Maxwell Perkins. In his office upstairs overlooking Fifth Avenue, he had charmed the best from Hemingway, Fitzgerald, Thomas Wolfe and Alan Paton. I read and reread their books with regularity.

Behind my barber chair was a wall of antique cameras, a banjo I never learned to play and original artwork from magazine illustrators I had worked with: Barron Storey, Bruce McCall and Ken Dallison. I prized the original drawing of Tennessee Williams which Linda Kalman had drawn for a *Playbill* cover.

In a closet-sized space was the kitchen which consisted of a half sink and an under-the-counter refrigerator. The bedroom contained a double bed with an unattached brass headboard and a small table on which my old Smith-Corona portable typewriter sat beside a 1920s oak filing cabinet.

♦

On a Saturday in September, I was sitting in the barber chair reading a letter David sent from Algeria. I read it through twice, surprised that he had written at all, and even more surprised at the ending. He closed it saying: "Give my regards to your father when you get to Mathews and tell him that, should she be willing, I look forward to taking his daughter to dinner when I get back. Take care, Apostle of Joy."

I didn't know what Apostle of Joy was supposed to mean and didn't know how to respond, and while flattered that he had written, I was wary of encouraging a long-distance romance. I put the letter in my filing cabinet alongside others from inaccessible men, mostly college friends. Two months later, David's mother sent me a small box of Christmas presents to give to him when he came back to New York.

I so liked Phoebe and Tony, and Phoebe had trusted me with an introduction to her son. She wouldn't have sent the presents had she not wanted me to see him again. Though I responded to her, I did not write back to him.

He showed up in June.

David was back working at the Landegger home office in the Pan-Am building, just a few underground corridors away from my office on Madison between 44th and 45th. Karl F. Landegger, the Austrian founder, had died the year before, and his sons, Carl and George, were running the company.

When David called, he was engaging on the phone. He said he really wanted to see me. His deep, gentle laugh was enticing. Would I join him for lunch in the Pan Am building that day?

At noon, I found my way through the underground tunnels and wound up on the elevator going up to the restaurant. I had no expectations other than that we might have a nice lunch.

He was waiting for me by the door, grinned, and, when the maître d' showed us to a table, David took my arm, then he seated me.

He ordered a Bloody Mary. Again I had a Dubonnet. He looked at me warmly, leaned across the table and said, "I've leased an apartment in Kips Bay, and bought a couch and some dishes. I'm having a little trouble believing how easy it is to walk into a store and come out with what I want—reverse culture shock, I guess. But it's nice to be back in a city full of good bars."

I found the remark about the bars strange, and wondered how much time he spent in pubs, drinking, picking up women.

I changed the subject and talked about what was going on at the agency. "A guy in the office has this dumb idea about a scratch 'n sniff promotion for Beecham. He wants consumers to describe the smell of Aqua Fresh toothpaste. I think it smells like toothpaste."

The corners of his mouth rose, his eyes sparkled, then he said: "Scratch and Sniff was very popular in Algeria." He paused. "Mostly in elevators." I laughed out loud.

That day I began to understand that, while he would never be ambidextrous, David had an ambidextrous mind. He juxtaposed thoughts with a result that was usually irreverent, astute and very funny. Was he opinionated? Oh, yes. Outrageous? Sometimes. But he seemed to know a good deal about a wide variety of subjects. And, just like his parents, he was refreshingly unpretentious.

♦

I realized I wanted to spend more time with David. I liked him. He was fun to be with, and he seemed to want to see me. But why was he only inviting me out at noon?

At our third lunch, a Friday, this time over blue points at the Oyster Bar in Grand Central Station, I said: "I never have a chance to linger over lunch. Today I have to rush back to meet a deadline for a radio commercial for Hamm's beer. Do you think you could invite me out for a dinner date?"

He cocked his head as if contemplating a very serious question. "Would you like that?" he asked. I nodded. We settled on the following Wednesday night. Only later did I realize it was the thirteenth of July, the third anniversary of PK's death. But I had said yes to David, and I had begun to understand that, while maybe it was not enough, I had given PK all God allotted for me to give.

While the past always played a role in the present, perhaps, after all, it need not remain in the starring role.

Chapter Nine

Let me tell you
what I was given, yes given—
provided, tendered, handed—
not in any sense
of the word, earned:
partner, friend

you turned
me on, twisted
my switch,
offered me nothing less
than life rekindled,
afire with all
its quaking brilliance.

That Wednesday evening before meeting David I had an appointment after work for drinks with a magazine publisher at the King Cole Bar at the St. Regis. I had completed an assignment for him, an interview with Buddy Rich, "the world's greatest drummer". I assumed he had other articles in mind.

The meeting included two Manhattans, a new assignment, a job offer to edit a small magazine in the Midwest (which I turned down on the spot, knowing it would be a giant step backwards). Mercifully, he skipped the usual semi-serious out-of-towner's attempt to bed me. From the hotel I took a cab down to 27th Street. Around 7:30 I walked into David's sparse but charming Kips Bay bachelor pad for the first time. It had a proper galley kitchen, a small living room and sleeping loft. I promptly fell asleep on his comfortable navy and white sofa.

He finally roused me. I apologized, and we headed to Once Upon A Stove, a restaurant on Third Avenue. Around 9:00, we had just settled into a table for two by the window and started looking at the menu when the lights flickered. They only flickered once, but David said: "Blackout. Come on. I know a place where there's a gas grill."

He grabbed my hand and we ran into the street to flag a cab which took off toward the West Village.

The ride down was harrowing, as there was still a good deal of traffic. With the street lights out, pedestrians, cars and cabs and buses were all jockeying to cross the intersections. Yet we arrived there within ten minutes.

Candles lined the bar where a dozen people sat hunched over drinks, and several candles lit each of the tables. The restaurant section in the rear was nearly empty. We sat down and began a quiet, leisurely dinner of strip steaks, salads and a half bottle of Bordeaux.

Though the city was in the middle of a fierce heat wave, the dark restaurant was comfortable. Below us, people were stuck in the subway. Above us, in nearby buildings, people were wedged into unmoving elevators and, at that moment, uptown in the Bronx and over in Brooklyn the heat-stressed and financially-depressed residents in no less than thirty-one neighborhoods had just begun a night-long rampage of arson and looting. Some seventy-five stores in Crown Heights were being looted, and two blocks of Broadway near Bedford-Stuyvesant in Brooklyn were ablaze. Fifty new cars were hotwired and stolen from a Bronx Pontiac dealer. Before morning, over 1,600 stores would be damaged and over 3,000 looters would be in jail. Mayor Abe Beame would call it "the night of terror".

Yet we were in a peaceful place having a fine dinner, thanks to a man who knew where there was a gas grill.

By the time we left, the bar was three deep in people. And the streets were emptying out. Occasionally, when the dim light of the night sky was shadowed by the taller buildings, it was difficult to see the sidewalk in front of us. The only lights were from the cars slowly passing by. None were cabs with a lit "vacant" sign. We began to walk.

I started to cross from Eighth Avenue onto 14th street, but David held me back. "Let's cross at 16th," he said. Immediately I understood. Fourteenth was wide, a street of large shops which could attract looters. Sixteenth was quieter, mostly residential. As we tuned into 16th Street, we came upon a gray-haired woman using a cane. She stopped suddenly, turned and looked at us. Even in the dark I could see distrust in her eyes.

We passed her, then David stopped and stood aside and looked back at her. He lit his cigarette lighter. "It's kind of dark out here," he called out. "Are you okay? Would you like us to walk with you for a while?

She shook her head. "I'm okay," she said. "You two go on."

"Do you have many flights to walk up?" he asked. She didn't respond.

We slackened our pace and turned around from time to time to check on her until she disappeared into the darkness. I hoped she had turned into a building half way up the block, and that her apartment was on the first floor.

At some of the major cross streets, people were helping to direct traffic. We stopped at South Park and 24th, and I played traffic cop for a few minutes. When the traffic slowed, David ran into the middle of the street, took my hand and hauled me off onto the sidewalk. "We have blocks to go before we sleep," he said. We kept walking.

In the dark, unable to see their distinguishing brick or concrete, the staunch mid-rise buildings on both sides of Park Avenue South melded into a single wall until lit up by a car creeping by. Ahead of us the Pan Am building was a dark block against the dim glow of the night sky.

When we tuned onto 35th Street and arrived at my building, I fully expected David to leave me at my front door, but he followed me in, lit his cigarette lighter again and opened the door to the stairs. And then he began to walk with me up nine flights. At the fourth floor landing, he stopped and bent down to kiss me. "Right here, in the middle of a blackout?" I asked. He laughed, kissed me anyway, and we kept climbing the stairs.

I opened both deadbolts with my keys. David lit the old kerosene lanterns I had bought at an antique store while visiting a friend near Sturbridge, Massachusetts. I collapsed on my couch and, within seconds, thanks to the drinks, followed by the wine, followed by the long walk, not to mention the late hour after a full day's work, I fell asleep again.

When I awoke an hour later, David was lounging in the barber chair reading Thor Heyerdal's *Kon Tiki.*

Who was this man, this *gentleman,* who, rather than take advantage of the night, of me, had seen me home safely and was quietly watching over me—and reading by gas light?

We kissed goodnight, and he left to walk downtown to his apartment. When he called the next day, he said he had stopped in a bar then continued home safely, and, since he had water and I did not, would I like to come by for a shower?

I would. I did. No, we did not shower together.

Chapter Ten

Believe
that from this trough
of melancholy I will swim
hard enough to break
above the waves,
arise,
unlock my fist,
turn my wrist,
and in my palm
gently cradle the remnants
of our love

Three months before the Blackout of 1977, Abe Hirschfeld had bought 15 and 17 Park Avenue, a single rent-stabilized building with separate entrances and separate hallways. Number 15 faced the avenue and Number 17 faced 35th Street. Without regard for or consent from the rent commission, he began to create a single entrance at 15 Park Avenue. A number of employees would lose their jobs, and there would be decreased security for the residents. The tenants were also beginning to become suspicious that his ultimate goal was to turn the building into a cooperative. With a mixture of elderly and young working singles, few of us could afford to purchase our apartments then pay the monthly maintenance fees.

Hirschfeld was a parking garage tycoon from Poland via Israel. He made a fortune building and managing numerous multi-story open-air garages throughout the city. At the same time, he frequently entered and lost public elections— for City Council, Manhattan Borough President, Lieutenant Governor of New York, Comptroller, even Mayor of Miami Beach.

In 1974 he ran for the U.S. Senate as "Honest Abe" and lost to Ramsey Clark in the Democratic primary. Later he would buy the bankrupt *New York Post*, which led to a staff revolt and a headline over his picture, saying "Who Is This Nut?" Hirschfeld fired then (under a court order) rehired editor Pete Hamill and, two weeks later, the paper was repurchased by Rupert Murdoch.

In 1998, Hirschfeld would offer a million dollars to Paula Jones to drop her sexual harassment lawsuit against President Bill Clinton. In 2000, he would be convicted of initiating a murder-for-hire plot against Stanley Stahl, a business partner. He spent only two years in prison, part of that time along with Godfather John Giotti and John Lennon's killer, Mark David Chapman—and also David Berkowitz, The Son of Sam.

Back in the mid 'seventies, Abe Hirschfeld simply seemed to be a brash man who, to a group of tenants at 15 and 17 Park Avenue, could not be trusted to follow regulations or tell the truth.

David spent the first hour and a half of our second date with a screwdriver and wrench, hunkered beneath the illegal reception desk Abe Hirschfeld erected at the 15 Park Avenue entrance. Hirschfeld had neither applied for a building permit nor advised the rent commission of his plans for the building. David was carefully disassembling the desk with the help and encouragement of dozens of tenants in the lobby.

Lou, the lawyer, and Harold, a mild-mannered shoe company executive, were carting off the dismantled pieces and stacking them in a corner. The elderly lady with the veiled hat was there (in her hat) sweeping up the dust.

When the police showed up, I pulled out the court order proving that the tenants had permission to remove the desk. They smiled and left. The desk was gone by 8:30 that night.

David and I went down to the Guardsman, had a drink, a sandwich, and played a round of darts. He won.

Actually, I felt as if I had won. I was with a man I was beginning to believe I could love.

He spent this night helping me, never questioning the task or demurring from what had to be done. He had simply slid under the desk and quietly gone to work.

A few days later, Sunday afternoon, the 17th of July, we went to the movies and saw *The Spy Who Loved Me*. It wasn't until we came out of the theater that he turned to me, took my hand, stopped in the middle of the sidewalk and said, "Today's my birthday."

At that moment it struck me that, as self-confident, as content as he seemed, David was very much alone. He had a mother and father he respected, a brother just sixteen months his senior, five children whom he talked about with a poignant tenderness, but were kept from him through circumstances he said neither he nor the court created; circumstances he did not choose.

Did he get through Christmas, his birthday, their birthdays reliving memories of better years, remembering them through the many photographs he had taken of them; pictures he no longer had?

Did he look forward to better years to come? I hoped so. Could I become a part of those years? Maybe so.

He had been in New York only a short time; before that in Algeria, Chicago, Richmond, Kalamazoo and Boston. He spoke fondly of a family he had befriended in Algeria and some colleagues in Chicago. Was I the only one in all of New York to know today was his birthday?

We passed a shop with an ice cream counter. I bought him a double-dip chocolate Haagen Dazs in a sugar cone and told the server to add extra carob sprinkles. "Happy Birthday," I said. He smiled. "Thanks."

We clicked cones. "A toast to you," I said. "Here's to your forty-first year."

♦

We spent the next few weekends roaming the city with our cameras. Both of us owned the same Canon SLRs; we swapped lenses on occasion; took pictures of Ellis Island, Coney Island, South Street Seaport, the lower East Side, Little Italy, the Battery. In those days Coney Island was about as dirty, derelict, raunchy and menacing as a city beachfront can be with tattered boardwalk games like "The Toilet Seat" ball toss; the "Bump Your Ass Off" bumper cars and the rumbling, wobbly Tornado roller coaster. The Battery wasn't much better. Both were filled with bums and near bums, men and women alike.

During those weeks I began to understand more about David's mission in Algeria. He was alone much of the time when he wasn't working and had begun to feel like a recluse. His living conditions were sparse. There was an ever-present potential for political unrest while the National Charter was drafted for Algeria's new constitution and the Western Sahara was being formed into a government in exile. Even so, he had embraced the job, championing the predominately Sunni-Muslim workers in the mill. He wanted them to succeed in an ambitious industrial project. He felt it was significant work.

His previous job in Chicago had left him with no extra income. His salary in Algeria supported him and his five children, which was one of the primary reasons he had gone overseas. His enthusiasm for the work kept him there.

During the course of those few weeks, we ate in the last Horn & Hardart automat in mid-

Manhattan, putting four quarters into a slot and opening the door beside it to pull out a dry cheese sandwich. We had better meals in numerous delis, uptown and down, at the 21 Club, Peter Lugers, and a fish restaurant in Brooklyn. We dropped in for a drink at Once Upon A Stove, at The White Horse Tavern, where Dylan Thomas' spirit still lingered, and at a number of dart pubs, including the Lion's Head and the Guardsman. One day I fixed a picnic which we ate on a bench overlooking the East River. I made my magical fried chicken—ready-made Swanson's reheated with paprika and chervil—and he kindly told me it was terrific.

I was attracted by so many aspects of him, like the way he often walked, James Dean style, with his shoulders hunched forward a bit and his head ducked down, contemplative, or how he'd turn a half turn, looking back, while moving forward. Sometimes he looked at me with scrunched-up eyes and his head cocked in a "what'cha talking about?" look.

I loved the way he smiled. As his expressive mouth turned up, his eyes often closed slightly, his whole face crinkling into a playful grin. Most of all I loved how he made me laugh. If I attributed too much importance to something trivial, he would put it into perspective with a gentle joke.

"Do you know that, if we got married, you'd become S.S. which would entitle you to fly a Panamanian flag and have your name painted across your ass?"

He was easy with a wide spectrum of humankind, from waiters and cab drivers to the wealthy, and he was comfortable with my assortment of friends: writers, artists, publishers and rising executives.

David was born in Bayside, Queens, NY. During World War Two, when his father was at sea, he, his mother and brother lived with his mother's family in Kew Gardens, Queens, and he started kindergarten at PS 99. After the war, the family moved to the secluded community of Scott's Cove in Darien, Connecticut, where they lived next door to Charles and Anne Morrow Lindberg and their five surviving children.

We had a running joke about the famous people we had met. The joke always ended with David saying, "Yes. But have you been in their living room?"

He saw more in our surroundings than I did. He opened up my world to boats and tides and the workings of so many things I took for granted. If he didn't know an answer, he sometimes made it up, then admitted he had made it up, but he was generally close enough to the truth to be believable. Next time the subject came up, David almost always knew more than he did before.

He was far from flamboyant, sometimes even quiet; sometimes gregarious and sometimes a little shy. He surprised me often. He would give me an unusual gift, like a hooded Algerian robe, or tell me he wanted to spend the day somewhere it had never occurred to me to go—like Coney Island. David was simply who he was and did not

99

pretend to be anyone else. I was endeavoring to become authentic, but he seemed to be truly authentic—without even trying.

I began to realize that, with most of my friends, after I got to know them fairly well, I could anticipate what they might say in most situations. Never with David. He was quickly becoming the most interesting man I had ever known. In addition, just like during the night of the blackout, I felt safe with him. He was strong and smart, and I sensed that he always had a reliable back-up plan.

In some respects, it was due to his native intelligence, but was enhanced by the fact that he had to learn at a young age how to compensate for restricted use of one hand. He had to reason through how he would hold a book, wrap a package or toss a tennis ball in a serve or do any one of the other thousands of tasks most of us do without thinking.

And yet, there appeared to be nothing he couldn't do.

Many years later he wrote to his grand-daughter, Tommi: "In late August of 1943, I fell out of a tree while on a plane spotting mission and crushed a good part of my left arm. I spent a few weeks in Flushing Hospital to avoid amputation due to gangrene. There were sulfur drugs but no antibiotics. The pain killer was aspirin ground up in orange juice. A defining moment in character and personality development, not all necessarily good, but there it was and is.

"I missed second grade entirely. At that time my father was a radio officer in the merchant marines, carrying aviation fuel to our allies. I depended on my mother or brother for anything requiring two hands.

"It took me months to learn how to tie my shoes with one hand, and I remember working at it for hours. Cutting food was another tough one. But it was the beginning of figuring things out and looking ahead to possible situations that might cause trouble."

♦

In early August, Parsons & Whittemore sent David on a mission throughout the U.S. to find a cement pipe plant company to buy for the son of Carl Landegger, one of his bosses. David joked about the triviality of the assignment, but took on the task with diligence. I returned from a business trip to California with a cold which turned into bronchitis. He called every night. He sent me postcards, each intentionally tackier than the last: the Crossroads Shopping Center in Waterloo, Iowa; the Greater New Orleans Bridge rising above a jumble of factories; the large but unremarkable U.S. post office in Columbia, S.C. On the back of a post card from Memphis, he wrote: "Just a cheerful reminder of ole Memphis, home of Dixie Belle, Holiday Inn, W.C. Handy, Beale Street and Quality Concrete Products."

Though Parsons & Whittemore had projects developing in a number of locations across the world, I never imagined that the home office was only a temporary place for David to park. He had a lease on an apartment which he had furnished.

While he claimed that, since his divorce, he was on a no-assets program, and was proud of the fact that he could travel through life with one suitcase, he had bought necessary furniture, pots and kitchen utensils plus two, but only two, tastefully masculine Dansk plates, cups and saucers and a two-place setting of flatware.

A few days after he returned from Memphis, David came by my apartment to pick me up for dinner. I sat in the barber chair, and he sat on the sofa sipping a Scotch.

He lowered his head, rubbed the back of his neck, then looked up at me, his demeanor thoughtful and his voice quiet, tentative: "I met with George Landegger today."

I leaned forward in the chair. "And?"

He took a sip of his Scotch, laid the drink on the coffee table and hesitated before swallowing and clearing his throat, as if to prepare a path for the words to follow: "I told George that I wanted the Nigerian job."

"Nigeria? Africa?" He nodded and smiled sheepishly. "The very one."

I leaned back in the chair, feeling the distance grow between me and the man I had just begun to believe I might trust myself to love.

It was as if I were watching a movie and would soon emerge from a dark theater into sunlight, and none of what I had just seen or heard would be real.

I took in a deep breath, held it, let it out. "And what did George say?"

David looked closely at me, his face searching mine. "I think I have a very good chance of getting it."

I felt my hopes tumble down into the old pit in my stomach which Dad had hollowed-out and PK had carved a little deeper.

Finally I went over to the couch, sat down next to David and leaned against his chest. He put his arm around me. When I could speak, I said: "I think I love you. And I want nothing more than to be with you."

"I know," he said. "I feel the same way about you." I looked up, and he smiled again—delicately, reflectively, a smile that told me that I could trust him; that I could learn to love him more than I had ever loved anyone before.

I hesitated, then my next words emerged, measured but uncensored, unplanned: "You need to do what is important to you," I said.

He drew me toward him and held me for a long time. He told me it was a start-up newsprint mill in the Calabar region of Nigeria. He'd be responsible for creating a viable industry in an impoverished region still suffering from the effects of the Biafran war.

When I finally pulled away and looked at him again, I felt that I could love those eyes, that mouth, that delicate, tantalizing smile—forever. But I knew I had not yet earned the right to claim that love. And there was more: if I truly respected him, how could I keep him from pursuing his dreams?

"You need to be who you are meant to be, not what I want you to be," I said.

They were the hardest words I had ever spoken. But they were the right words. If he left, I might never see him again. But even if, somehow, I convinced him to stay, I would lose more. I would lose the very essence of what I wanted to love about this man.

Chapter Eleven

Mary Magdalene
late at night
upon a stage
of my imagining,
her torment, mine,
the incessant
drumming: I love,
I want, I just don't know
what to believe.

Together we read what we could about Nigeria.
David would live in Lagos, a former slave port
and the capitol at that time. There he could deal
with the banks and the Ministry of Industries
and the suppliers, including Fougerolle, the
French engineering company in charge of
constructing the mill.

What we read about Lagos in 1977 wasn't
pretty: impossible traffic, mass confusion,
corruption, a succession of governments ending
in coups, and a bribery system that pervaded
nearly every aspect of everyday life. Wages were
low; life expectancy was low; infant mortality,
poverty and crime were among the highest in the
world.

Today the Federal Government has moved to
the thoroughly modern planned city of Abuja,

but Lagos has continued to grow to some fifteen million people. Today there are enclosed shopping malls, new high-rise offices, modern restaurants serving food of all nationalities. A mass transit rail system is in the works. It is a changing city. In 1977 it was overflowing with minimally-educated subsistence farmers looking for work in a newly oil-rich nation. Unable to deal with the influx, the city of Lagos was in chaos.

The newsprint mill was to be constructed in Oku Iboku, a village in the Calabar region where the Biafran War had recently been fought. The London office in charge of the project, Parsons-Whittemore-Lyddon, had, to date, invested several million dollars, yet none of their invoices were currently being paid. David's job was to get them paid and move the venture closer to getting started.

Larger companies with projects abroad employed a staff combined of expatriate and local workers, and provided a housing compound for the expatriates. David would have only a small Nigerian staff at his disposal and would live alone in a house which contained a temporary office. London would send visiting financial, legal and engineering personnel as needed.

When David vacated his apartment at the end of August, he put all he owned in storage, and packed one large suitcase for a potential two-year stay in Nigeria. But before he left, he treated me to a quiet and elegant New York weekend. George Landegger agreed to foot the bill.

David was scheduled to leave on Sunday, September Fourth, the day before Labor Day. We took Friday afternoon off and walked past the gold and frescoed ceilings of the elegant rotunda to the registration desk at The Pierre.

The Pierre is a grand hotel at the corner of 61st Street and Fifth Avenue. Its forty-two stories rise from a limestone Louis XIV base; the top floors are modeled after Mansart's baroque chapel at Versailles. It was built by Charles Pierre Casalasco, a busboy from Corsica who immigrated to New York and was trained as a restaurateur by Louis Sherry. His hotel venture was backed by Wall Street financiers Otto Kahn, E. F. Hutton and Walter P. Chrysler, among others.

In October, 1930, the Pierre opened with a gala dinner prepared by none other than the great chef, August Escoffier.

The Pierre was later owned by John Paul Getty. In 1977 it was being managed by the English company, Trust House Forte. *Architectural Record* editor William Weathersby Jr. called the Pierre "the discreet society sister of the Plaza and the Waldorf." Elizabeth Taylor, Harrods owner Mohamed al-Fayed and Yves Saint-Laurent have all owned private residences in the hotel.

Our small but comfortable room overlooked Central Park and the city beyond. I'd packed the fanciest clothes that I owned—a Diane von Furstenburg wrap dress purchased one Sunday morning on Hester Street for a tenth the going price, a teal sheath with matching coat which cost me half a paycheck on sale at Lord & Taylor and a pair of yellow and red striped bell bottoms. I vowed that, to make it seem like the special occasion it was, I would not go south of 57th Street all weekend. I would play the part of a woman of means rather than that of a working girl.

We talked. We laughed. We cheered each other up. And we stayed above 57th Street all weekend.

I gave David a brown leather briefcase I had bought at Ambassador Luggage on Madison Avenue. He gave me a pair of earrings, gold strands woven into intricate balls. On my business trip to California a few weeks before, I'd finally given in to having my ears pierced and was still wearing the piercing studs.

On Friday night after dinner, we went up to the Carlyle on East 65th Street for drinks and to hear the stunning music of blind jazz pianist George Shearing. I had been to the Carlyle several times to hear Bobby Short, who regularly played there. Short was enjoyable; Sir George was sophisticated, mellow, silky. He played his vibrant composition, *Lullaby of Birdland*, at times both of his hands striking the melody in parallel to caper with authentic jazz, then he paused only briefly and, as if to flood the brimming love I was feeling for the man sitting next to me, he played *I Only Have Eyes for You*. When he played the first slow treble notes of *Tenderly* with a teasing mix of fancy and passion, I was close to agony knowing I only had one more day to spend with David.

◆

On Saturday we walked up Fifth Avenue to the Metropolitan Museum to see the African collection, and paid close attention to the lost-wax bronzes which originated in the 13th century in Benin, a former kingdom in southwest Nigeria. When we came out, we walked north, stopping to watch the model boats sail across the Central Park conservatory.

We walked back downtown through the park, holding hands, and sat on a bench outside the zoo to eat Sabrett hot dogs from a near-by cart, David's with sauerkraut, mine with grilled onions. While we ate, we talked.

"I don't have any status on the job yet," he said. "I just don't know where it will lead. When I've figured it out, I want us to be together. I really do."

He turned and faced me, held my chin in his hand and looked directly into my eyes. "I just can't believe how well suited we are for one another." He smiled. "I can't believe how much I love you."

I wanted—oh, how I wanted—to believe him, but he was headed half way around the world, and I knew by then how evanescent love could be. Realistically, we might be spending our last full day together.

I took his hand from my chin, rubbed it against my cheek and reached over and kissed him. He smiled. "Right here in Central Park?"

"Yes, right here in Central Park."

That afternoon we had tea at the Plaza. We skipped dinner. He called his children and his parents, then we went down to the Café Pierre to hear the Hungarian pianist Tony Gorody.

We held onto each other through the night, knowing it would be a long time—if ever—before we could do so again.

On Sunday I stood at the bottom of the long red-carpeted ramp watching David climb the steep incline to board Pan Am Flight 100 to London. He would spend a few days at the office in the London suburb of Croydon before going to Lagos. He walked slowly with his head hunched forward, his new briefcase bulging, heavy at his side. Toward the top he turned, looked at me, smiled a little contrite smile—then disappeared into the darkness behind the ramp.

I stood there a few minutes, picturing him again and again walking up that bright red carpeted incline and hoping he would reappear. Then I went to a nearby window and waited until the 747 finally backed out. The noise of the engines was muffled through the window, and as the plane taxied to the runway, the sound faded away, like a love song drawing to a melancholy close.

I shivered and wandered out of the airport in a daze. I felt stranded, entirely alone.

♦

Thanks to one of my clients, I had tickets to the U.S. Open in Forest Hills, the last of the three years that matches were played on their clay courts. I took a cab from the airport and met Norbert outside the stadium. He was an avid tennis fan, and, for all the support he had given me at Scribner's and at *Flying*, I was pleased to be able to treat him to an afternoon at the Open.

That year Chris Evert won her seventh Grand Slam title against Wendy Turnbull, and Guillermo Vilas defeated Jimmy Connors in four sets. But the big event was the women's doubles. The year before, Renee Richards (formerly Richard Raskind) had been denied entry into the tournament due to a sex change. In 1977 the Supreme Court ordered the USTA to permit her to play, but Richards and Betty-Ann Stuart lost to Martina Navàrtilová and Betty Stöve.

Norbert may have been watching tennis; I was still watching David walk up that long, red-carpeted ramp. Norbert may have been listening to the thunk of the ball against the clay. All I heard was David's voice. When the players took a break between games and we could talk, I did all the talking; Norbert did not even have a chance to respond with one of his famous puns.

And there was only one subject I wanted to talk about: the wonderful, incomparable, extraordinary and astonishing David Stiles. My obsessive talk was because I felt I loved him as much as a person can love someone they have known for less than two months; it was also because I needed confirmation. Was he really the extraordinary man I thought he was?   Or was he, at least, extraordinarily right for me?

Chapter Twelve

Once upon
a time,
before thumbs fluttered
across each mindless
moment, described every bite
of today's peanut butter
sandwich, posted each
clichéd cliché to a thousand
bbfs, there was an hour

of twilight
to stroll across the street, chat
f2f across
an uneven row of pickets,
return to
an uncluttered table,
light a pale lamp and write
in languid long-hand

about the wondrous
and perplexing, the satisfying
and vexing. To write
I love you
in a hundred different ways.

Today Maasai in Kenya or Tanzania tend their goats while talking on cell phones. A Blackberry lab is being built in Lagos.

In the Lagos of 1977 there were no cell phones, no satellites, no email or personal computers. I could not reach David by phone because he didn't even have a landline. The Nigerian telephone system was so primitive and phones so rare and unreliable that few Nigerians and even fewer expatriates in Lagos bothered to have telephones. To call me or the office in London, David stood in a long line at a NET office behind others trying to call overseas—provided the phone system was even working. The wire system was more reliable, though a cable often took days to be delivered.

We could send letters either direct to Lagos or through the London office. Direct could take ten days to two weeks. Through London, it depended upon whether or not someone was scheduled to go to Lagos or through Lagos to the site. Before he left, David brought me his stereo system with a turntable and tape recorder with dubbing capabilities. He added a stack of romantic music tapes. I promised him that this time I would write, and I would cut him some tapes as well.

The evening after David departed London for Lagos I put on the red and blue striped cotton shirt he left with me and wrote him my first letter—full of the doubts and questions I had pushed aside during our brief but so-exciting courtship.

"This morning I looked for you standing behind me in the mirror, but you were missing. Still, I told you that I loved you. When I turned around and reached up and pretended to straighten your tie, everything felt okay again. But then the day went on and, by the time you had arrived in Lagos, it had become almost impossible to reach up and straighten your tie.

"I asked you a question, but nobody answered. Even still, I asked you another one, then another—all these questions suddenly important because I could no longer see you— your face, your smile, which always douses the flickering doubts arising in my mind. I wondered if I was wrong about you. Was I wrong?

"So here are the questions: Are you running away from disappointment? From me? Do you pick up strange women? Do you fall in and out of love in a hurry? I don't think so, but would you please send me a quick list of your bad habits so I can love you properly? Otherwise I'll be forced into inventing such characteristics to make you seem real—and that hardly seems fair. Hurry! I've already invented four or five. Hurry! I just invented another one."

"It would also help if you'd get mad at me, or be just a little irrational. Otherwise I can't properly judge my feelings. See what two days apart can do to me? Oh, my. I think I really ought to spend some time with you as soon as possible, especially if during that time you could get mad at me."

And I continued to write: "But it was all insane. We were pushing too fast. Most of all don't reread this letter. If I send it, it will be against my better judgment. But I told you that after you left I'd feel confused. Not to mention left. I do.

"I miss you totally.
Whoever you are.
I love you totally.
Whoever you are."

♦

Before I joined Dancer-Fitzgerald-Sample, I was under the impression that advertising people would be smarter and worldlier than I was. Many of them were, but this elite group of serious account executives and highly creative artists and writers made me feel welcome and confident. They brought us such classics as the Energizer bunny, the Mars candy commercial, "Sometimes You Feel like a Nut", Toyota's "O, What a Feeling!" and "Our L'eggs fit your legs". By 1978, L'eggs pantyhose packaged in the famous egg had become the number one brand of hosiery. Later, they also produced "Where's the Beef?" for Wendy's. They worked long hours at a fervent pace—and so did I.

I had begun to develop a solid relationship with a few of our clients, including L'eggs, Toyota and the Arby's franchise owners. Arby's, which was growing at the rate of fifty stores a year, had been promoting their restaurants through two-for-one coupons, which created a surge of customers during the couponing periods but did nothing to help their image. We sold them on several promotions, including a December campaign featuring attractive Currier & Ives winter scenes on a series of collectible glasses which would create return traffic and help to upgrade the restaurant's image.

In addition, I was meeting almost weekly with the building tenants and nearly as often with Abe Hirschfeld in his office or in court to try to negotiate necessary maintenance and upgrades while keeping the phones and elevator service as they were—and fighting his (still vehemently denied) goal of turning the building into a co-op.

My Puerto Rican student, Timmy, was steadily improving his reading ability, and I would return home from our early evening sessions inspired to take him to the next level. Soon he would graduate from *The Reader's Digest* to full-length books. He wouldn't spend his whole life working in a warehouse.

While I often joined friends for dinner, perhaps a show, went to the movies, attended sporting events or special functions, what I remember most about the autumn of 1977 was sitting in my office long after sundown writing a letter to David—or sprawling on the floor beside the tape machine in my living room dubbing funny stuff mixed with romantic music into tapes I sent off to him.

On the thirteenth of September I wrote David again and closed the letter saying, "I want you to be there doing what you need to do more than I ever wanted anything for anybody, but, at the same time, I also want to be with you, feeling the

117

good feeling that you are, wanting to know for sure if I could live with you for a long, long time."

My fervent and ever-present question had become: were we really right for each other, or had these past six weeks been mere fantasy? Yet on September twentieth I wrote another letter which negated the one I had just sent. While I had no desire to date anyone else, neither did I want to spend more years chasing an ephemeral vision. And, since I had vowed that I would not play games with this romance, I told him exactly how I felt.

"The uncertainty, the illusions, the dreams or half-dreams, the fear of ultimate rejection— the whole thing is swimming around in my head and making me crazy.

"I need to know as soon as you know what's going to happen. Several times I've been on the verge of writing to you and saying we've got to stop pretending we have a future. I can't go through with the letters, the wondering, the waiting, the conjecture any more. I'd rather quit now and get on with life here—even though the alternatives may turn out to be less appealing."

◆

After writing several more letters, I finally received David's letters of September seventh and ninth in which he described his early days in Lagos. He had not yet received any of my letters. I followed up with yet another letter, a tape and a two-page list of my faults, including a few he must have recognized by then such as:

118

"I'm restless and impatient; mull over things a lot; can't hold problems in; use a lot of paper." And: "I am hopelessly in love with you."

What I neglected to mention was that I sometimes wrote dumb, obsessive letters

By the time he'd been gone for three weeks, I may have been totally confused, but he was not. He had a rational plan. I just didn't know what it was.

What he didn't have, couldn't have, was a schedule.

Chapter Thirteen

Market child,
don't run from me.
Listen.
This is true:
the ochre bones of our common story
lie deep below these wooden stalls.
You could be
my distant cousin's child.
You extend your saffron hands,
ask for candy. Your uncle
sells me nougats, keeps the change,
scratches a tumor
big as an onion on his jaw. I give
you nougats. Only nougats.
I want. You want.
So much more.

In a number of ways Nigeria suffered from the after-effects of sixty years of British colonialism. The British had drawn the country's boundaries for commercial and military reasons, ignoring indigenous lands. Over three hundred ethnic groups were called Nigerians, though they differed in language, culture, even basic physical features. Though English was the official language, most spoke a form of pidgin.

More than half of the population belonged to three powerful groups, each with their own strong political views and parties: the Islamic Hausa-Fulani in the north; the Igbo in the east; and the Yoruba, predominately in the southwest.

In 1966, regional hostilities escalated when Igbo officers assassinated the federal prime minister and the premiers of the Northern and Western regions. In retaliation, Igbos living in the North were massacred, leading to a complex and bloody series of events causing the Igbos to secede from the country and form the state of Biafra. The secession prompted the three-year civil war which ended in 1970, after some three million people had died from combat, hunger or disease.

By the early 1970s, reconstruction began in the Cross River State in Igbo territory, aided initially by Port Harcourt oil revenue. One of the plans was to build a newsprint mill and supporting township in Oku Iboku, a small village upriver from the town of Calabar. A forest of fast-growing gmelina trees, originally indigenous to India, had already been planted to produce pulp, and contracts were being let to build the town site and infrastructure such as the effluent plant, as well as the mill itself. The mill was to attract satellite businesses and become a commercial center within the country.

There are places on this earth where civilization's skin is so thin it can bleed out with the mere flick of a tyrant's fingertip or a rebel's sword. And yet there are those who venture into such places either to convert the inhabitants to their way of life; to exploit their rich resources, or to help provide the people with the dignity that comes with meaningful work.

In 1977, Lagos, Nigeria was such a place. David's mission was to provide its people with meaningful work.

♦

His first letter began: "From Sunday when I left you to Wednesday when I arrived here, it seemed as if a year had passed and, at the same time, I had slipped back several generations in time. Lack of staff, multiple lineless lines, oppressive heat and low ceilings made the two-hour customs process the worst I have ever been through. It was an honest prelude to my first day in Lagos."

He began his stay at the Maryland Guest House, where he slept on a too-short mattress crammed into a home-made frame. The lobby was a small room with a few dusty overstuffed chairs. The restaurant decor resembled the fourth-best diner in, say, Abilene, Kansas. Power was erratic.

"On the bright side," he wrote, "I'm feeling fine and smelling rather native, though a bucket of water has been promised for the morning."

David wrote that the former British managing director would carry this letter back to London having resigned from Parsons & Whittemore, Lyddon without telling the Nigerian government. David would move into the office and guest house in Ikeja where the former director had lived. "The house is guarded day and night," he wrote. "And steel bars cover all the doors and windows, though they are painted white to relieve the image of a prison."

The house was on Ikorodu Road, an expanding highway between the Murtala Muhammed International Airport and the Eko Bridge crossing into downtown Lagos. There were unending squat semi-finished (but occupied) cement block or wooden buildings behind a row of market stands lining each side of the road; no sidewalks; open sewers; unpaved side streets, and people constantly dodging a relentless stream of fast-paced traffic (all horns honking) to run across the highway. Not everyone made it.

"The crime rate is exceedingly high," he wrote. "Two blocks away, four bandits broke into a house to steal and, while there, they cut up one of the inhabitants. A mob stormed the house and killed the four bandits, then the mob got theirs from a second mob on their way out. Justice by machete."

David's job required him to be in the city center at the banks, suppliers or the Federal Ministry of Industries nearly every day. But because of the increasing number of cars in Lagos, because of the almost-constant "go-slow" around accidents, it sometimes took three or four hours to travel those 10 kilometers. Along the way, in the middle of the street, beggars begged and hustlers hustled. Boys and girls sold newspapers, steam irons, radios, peanuts, mothballs, yams, oranges, laundry soap—any products they could obtain to sell.

The government solved the traffic problem by mandating that even-numbered license plates would be allowed onto the mainland only on Monday, Wednesday and Friday, and odd-numbered license plates only on Tuesday, Thursday and Saturday. As a result, to do business on a daily basis, you simply needed two cars. It was a fine decision for Mercedes, Peugeot and Audi, but did nothing to ease congestion in Lagos.

"Everywhere you look are tin-roofed shacks, garbage piles, packed dirt, sewage—and poverty. Construction and squatting have removed most of the trees and tropical plants," he wrote.

"Embassy row faces the sea, but between the embassies and the shore are more hovels and litter and people—always the people. It looks like a perfect place to start a cholera epidemic.

"But the Nigerians must be basically honest, since the Ministry of Tourism is an incredible dump of a building—obviously owned by Abe Hirschfeld."

That September, the paper mill project, instigated by the Nigerian government to provide industry to the Cross River State, was in shambles. "We have not received any payment for services from the government since January. All equipment contracts are in default for lack of down payment. The management contract has not been signed. If we can't begin to clear the site, fifty people will lose their jobs."

He said that, due to the traffic, offices closing by 3:30 in the afternoon, and the former director's penchant for stopping for a beer

125

between appointments, "I have only been able to meet with three of the twenty-five or so people I need to see in order to get on with it.

"And since the end-of-Ramadan holidays begin this Friday afternoon, four days before they are supposed to begin, nobody will be available at the ministries or banks until next Thursday."

In 1977, the country's oil revenues had weakened due to soaring inflation in Nigeria and widespread corruption among those who skimmed the revenues for their own use. There was currently no money to support the mill or other pending projects, though the government was in the process of trying to float a four and a half billion dollar series of loans.

"This morning I met with the British High Commission and our exchange bankers to get the status confirmed and to try to determine if the mill is, in fact, slated to be built or dropped. Nobody knows for sure. No great sense of security pervades, and my two-year stay may last another week.

"Nigeria is the greatest unfinished country in Africa," he said. "Surely the woman I love has more sense than wanting to live here. I do love you and miss you very much."

Chapter Fourteen

slowly
I reread your letters
and tucked them, one by one
deep into the rifts
between each memory.

David knew that managing the construction of a town and mill in a jungle setting was a huge load to shoulder, but, at age forty-one, it was a job he was ready to tackle. I felt he was just the man to do it, and maybe I could even help him to succeed. While I loved my work, it was more like play than real work. Perhaps it was time to make a more worthy contribution, both to society and to one significant man. And yet I continued to question whether or not the slender thread of love stretching between New York and Lagos was strong enough to hold us until we could be together again.

After David received my first letter and tape, he responded.

"Dear Crazyperson: One of my bad habits is ignoring specific instructions, so I have reread your letter. I would have listened to the tape again, but Gibbs is sleeping with the cassette player—to each his own—but, after all, it is his.

"Most of my faults have disappeared since the night of the NY blackout, so you will not

127

receive a list. You tell me when I'm irrational. I'll get mad at you when it's called for, but I don't know why. I have picked up strange women and not picked up women who wanted to be picked up. I can't squat in yesterday's debris.

"Our love for each other is not insane but very natural, and it _is_ real and, finally, we did not push too fast; we wasted too much time being sure, and the less we waste from now on the more we'll have.

"If you are trying to get rid of me verbally it won't work because I love you. You can get rid of me by ceasing to care, and you won't have to say a word.

"Enough analysis, woman, enough! What I am, you're the rest of it, most of it, and it's all your fault and I love you. Good night.

"P.S. The Nigerian navy put out a request for bids for food for the year. The biggest single item was 340,000 kilos of yams."

♦

Four days later, he wrote again and enclosed a tape.

"Hello out there. I just finished throwing a bunch of darts with Tony Gibbs and, frankly, it made me sentimental, so I interrupted the competition to write to you. Fortunately I have not been drinking or I would throw myself under a mammy wagon, and you could sue the 'Smile On My Face Transit Company' for a fistful of Naira—almost $1.98.

"Yesterday I spent six hours in traffic and seven hours in the ministries with the visiting lawyer from London, getting nowhere and accomplishing nothing. Today was better: only four hours in traffic and four hours in the ministries accomplishing nothing.

"I have been here two weeks, and all I've seen is the slums and rear ends of cars, buses and motorcycles.

"Time is passing like a leaking faucet. It's been my fault, so it's my job to fix it. Maybe I can do it and still have a job."

He continued the letter a few nights later.

"I received a message from Landegger today instructing me to move into Lagos at either major hotel as a start on finding better housing on Victoria Island. That way I can avoid the traffic problem. Also, it will determine how soon and under what conditions you might join me here.

"Last night I wrote to the children and my parents and was going to send another off to you, but I have a new thing happening and decided to think about it overnight.

"For the first time I really don't want to be here, even though the work, money and experience are what would normally keep me happy. Not being with you and feeling the need of you constantly has made the trade too costly. If you were here, I know we'd see things I can't be bothered looking at alone.

"Not knowing what and how you're doing concerns me, not out of envy or jealousy or worry, but only because we belong to each other.

Everything seems pallid under the present circumstance.

"I will stay until my visa expires December 6th because I have made that much of a commitment to Landegger. But before the rest of the two-year decision is made, you and I are going to get on with us, and to hell with them, if that's what it takes.

"The commitment to you—or to us—doesn't carry any shadows with it of having to give anything up or any threats to individuality—yours or mine. We seem to function together better than we do alone. At least I do. If that's love, then I love you. If it's not love, then I *whatever* it is you, and I'm very happy about the whole thing."

The next day, I responded: "David, beautiful David, I received your tape last night. You have no idea how good it was to hear your voice; it was almost like talking to you. And then this morning there was your letter, and not just any letter, a book of a letter, and it's too much to respond to all at once. Wow, I love you, David. I love you more than I thought I could ever love anybody. I love how you think, how you write, how you talk, how you make me laugh.

"David Stiles is alive and well and living on this earth, and on top of that David Stiles says he loves me. If you only knew how good that makes me feel. If there was ever a man I could hope to envision alongside the woman I want to be, that man is you."

Chapter Fifteen

You, my confidante
on voyages back
and forth through time;
the splendid muse
who whispers
stories yet to write,
poems yet to rhyme.

September brought on the twinges of melancholy, as summer turned its back and ran from oncoming autumn winds.

I felt that I wanted to live in cotton forever, feel the sun knead my hair and polish my face. And when I rubbed the back of my neck, I wanted to see sweat glistening on my hand, a welcome gift from a long summer's day. I wanted David by my side, sharing lighthearted summer.

Today, thirty-five years later, as the first leaves begin to spiral down from the surrounding maple trees, I feel every bit as melancholic as I did in 1977.

I plug a small SanDisk drive into the USB port on my computer to let David's voice take me back and lift my heart no less than when I first listened to these words on a tape recorded many years ago.

"This poor old JVC 9310S carries voices back and forth; it doesn't know how to love somebody; doesn't know how to be loved by anybody; doesn't know how to feel alive; doesn't know god damn nothin'; I know all those things. I know I love you. And I am so excited about us I can hardly believe it. We're going to be okay; a mystery to the rest of the world. I hope. Boy, I hope.

"We're going to fool the universe; we'll be smiling so much they won't know what we're up to. We're up to each other.

"I love you. Oh, I love you.

"You are where it all happens, begins and ends for me, and I have to stay optimistic about what our life will be like. You are very loveable; it just takes someone as crazy as me to love you. You are also a very exciting person to be with, which is another reason I don't like being without you. I guess all I really want is everything."

♦

With each of David's letters and tapes, my feelings fluctuated from infatuation to deep caring to admiration to respect, back to infatuation, though in between I continued to question what the hell I was doing.

I needed a strong dose of faith to accept—like the bread and wine of communion—without further doubting, perpetually questioning, the love David was offering me.

As I study his early letters, I realize that he had continually, steadily, gently told me he loved me. He persistently said that, one way or another, we would be together again, though how and when that would happen was never a constant in the equation.

During his first several months in Lagos, dealing with a sluggish and unstable business environment in a tumultuous city, he was not even sure that the project would continue or that suitable housing for the two of us could be found or approved. He was currently living upstairs in his office, near town but, with the traffic, hours away from the central district. His expectations of when we might be together and where we might be living seemed to fluctuate with each letter. And while I wanted to be with him—immediately—I was not yet ready to marry him. After all, we'd only enjoyed six weeks of life together.

Significant men had evaporated from my life; the undying love of less-significant men proved to be considerably less than professed, or the men themselves were considerably less consequential than I originally assumed. Was it any wonder that I often doubted that David could unequivocally, unreservedly love me since we had only known each other for a short time, and he'd chosen to leave me some 7,000 miles behind?

Yet David had awakened in me a dormant capacity to care deeply about another human being.

While I told David often and in numerous ways that I loved him, I also laid bare my fears and my concerns about him, about the serious commitment I felt marriage required since divorce was not a choice I ever wanted to face. I also asked questions about the kind of life we might be living together in West Africa. In an atmosphere so different from New York, could I remain the productive woman I had worked hard to become?

At the same time I tried to entertain him with small gifts such as original cartoons, newspaper clippings and antique postcards. When I talked to him on tape, I dubbed in every fitting or funny sound I could find: *The Hallelujah Chorus*; Richard Nixon declaring "I am not a quitter" followed by "therefore I shall resign"; a children's recording of *Chicken Little* crying out "The sky is falling!" at in ever-increasing frenzy. I dubbed in a phone call to "dial a prayer" followed by a call to "dial a joke" and sent him Pete Seeger singing every single verse of *We Shall Overcome*. I sent him news of sporting events and elections, even excerpts from his childhood favorite, "The Green Hornet". Every tape ended with Barbra Streisand singing *Evergreen*. To me, the song captured exactly how I felt about us together—ever-astounding, ever-fresh.

Perhaps the distance that separated us, the lack of instant interaction, helped us both to communicate more thoughtfully, more honestly and even more passionately than we might have otherwise. Perhaps the long wait between letters gave us time to reflect more seriously than if we had access to cell phones, texting and Skype.

When there was a long gap between his letters, I worried about him and, at the same time, began to doubt that he cared about me enough. I sometimes felt that it would be wise to end this impossible romance. For instance, in October, I wrote: "Maybe I should change my thinking from hoping to see you soon to maybe seeing you some day."

Yet, each letter or tape I received was a prize—a new revelation, a small unveiling—that I read or listened to again and again. And for a little while, with each one, my reservations receded and I fell in love again.

David gave me what no man had ever given me before. If I was distressed, he would often calm me with humor. If restive, he would still me with his quiet composure. Of course, on occasion, one or both of us raised our voices in exasperation, but not very often.

I feel so blessed. I can experience those tapes and letters whenever I wish. Just today I came across the letter I received in October, 1977 in which he proposed marriage—uniquely in the manner of David Stiles. "We may have to get married on a sailboat tied to a tree at the Vail ski slopes with Abe Hirschfeld as best man and the local witch doctor in the pulpit, but I'm ready whenever you are."

Chapter Sixteen

If only
I could slice
through this fabric
of chicanery,
manipulating glue;
toss the prattle
with the rubbish—
and retain
one tiny precious seed
of truth.

Abe Hirschfeld, our new landlord at 15-17 Park Avenue, was a short, stocky man with a wide, doughy, unruly face and equally unruly hair, a wide mouth with a noticeable gap between his prominent two front teeth. In 1977, his hair was fringed with gray, and the skin beneath his eyes and chin were beginning to loosen and swell. He often bragged of his fifth-grade education, and spoke with Yiddish intonations that he himself called "an accent as thick as a slab of corned beef".

In Hirschfeld's 2003 autobiography, *Crazy and In Charge (As Told to Mark Ribowsky)*, he modestly claimed, among many other things, to have saved the economy of the USA three times; taught real estate to Donald Trump and Leona

Helmsley; "single-handedly elected" Jimmy Carter president and also brought about the election of Presidents Ronald Reagan and George W. Bush as well as Prime Minister Tony Blair. Hirschfeld also asserted that was a major player at the 1978 Camp David Accords which secured the Nobel Peace Prize for Anwar El Sadat and Menachem Begin. He also said he had written some 10,000 jokes.

Our fifty-year-old building on the corner of Park and 35th Street was built by Fred F. French, famous for his ornate art deco skyscraper on Fifth Avenue and for Knickerbocker Village, a middle-class development on the Lower East Side. Due to the poor move-in condition of Knickerbocker Village apartments, the tenants formed an association which organized a rent strike.

Ironically, the Knickerbocker Village protests apparently led to more stringent rent-control laws. Landlords who owned a building with rent-controlled or rent-stabilized apartments were required to comply with the regulations of the rent commission.

Just inside the 17 Park Avenue lobby—accessed from 35th Street—was an old-fashioned plug-in-the-wires switchboard linked to the apartments. The switchboard operator took messages, connected calls, screened visitors and alerted tenants when a guest was on the way up. The elevator was self-service. Most of the apartments were studio or one-bedroom units with kitchenettes and were primarily occupied by single residents, many of them older women.

More couples lived in the 15 Park Avenue full-kitchen apartments. The passenger elevator was manned 24 hours by an operator who served as the building's security.

Abe Hirschfeld's plan was to close the 35th Street entrance and remove the switchboard. All tenants would enter from 15 Park Avenue. To reach the unattended 17 Park Avenue elevator, tenants would walk down a newly-constructed long, narrow hallway. The manned elevator in 15 Park Avenue would become self-service, and one concierge would serve as security for both buildings.

Not long after David left, we were in the midst of a tenant meeting in my apartment. Lou the lawyer sat in the barber chair; Harold the shoe mogul and Lincoln the philosophy professor were hunkered down on the couch; Joshua, our young, socially-conscious lawyer, sat on the floor beside my plywood coffee table—painted a mahogany red at the time. I was in the kitchen, pouring Lou a beer, when I noticed a Rolls Royce pull up at the corner. A few minutes later, the doorbell rang; it was a young man from Hirschfeld's office. I invited him in and offered him a drink. I had a half bottle of budget Burgundy, a few cans of Busch beer and a couple of Cokes on hand.

"I'll have a Perrier," he said. I looked down on his dazzling new Italian shoes, up at his glossy, wide silk Hermes necktie, and said, "Right. Second choice?" He declined to make a second choice.

He said Hirschfeld wanted to work with us to create a safe, attractive building, but, after all, they had invested in an old, run-down structure, and should be allowed to improve it as he saw fit. Hirschfeld would be willing to settle out of court if we permitted him to make the changes he desired.

Joshua reminded him that we still held the restraining order for Hirschfeld's unpermitted attempt to build a reception desk and would be seeing him in court on October 9th to settle the matter legally.

With that we thanked him, ushered him out and continued with our meeting. We would allow Hirschfeld to settle out of court provided he fully restored the lobby and agreed to our stipulations for improvements to the building with no changes in security services—and paid our lawyer's fee

That fall Abe was running for city council. One of the tenants went to the local print shop and returned with signs for each of us to hang from our windows: "Vote No to Abe Hirschfeld." As ususal, Abe lost.

Carol Bellamy won the race in a runoff against Paul O'Dwyer. At the same time, the mayoral race for the "soul of the city" pitted ineffectual incumbent Abe Beam against brassy Bella Abzug as well as "How am I doin'?" Ed Koch and Liberal Party candidate Mario Cuomo. Koch won the city, though Cuomo was soon appointed lieutenant governor.

On Monday, the twelfth of September, I was invited to lunch with Abe. As I walked into the dark restaurant, Abe beckoned me to his table with a manic wave of both hands. "Dahlink", he said. "Beautiful Dahlink!" I sighed, ducked into the ladies room to gather myself against the charade I expected to follow, then slowly made my way to his table.

Over pastrami sandwiches every bit as thick as Abe's accent, we talked about the building.

"It's an old building," Abe said. We all knew it needed paint, some rewiring and re-plumbing. "I want to make it nice for you, but it costs a lot of money. I want to keep the building, but I'm losing too much money."

As a result of my lunch meeting, the tenant's committee began a negotiating process with Hirschfeld. He would provide us with plans for a larger, safer lobby conversion. Hirschfeld's office began to call me daily. What color rug would I like in the lobby? Did I prefer teak on teak or mahogany and brass elevator cabs? Naturally, if I wanted the fire door moved, it would be moved.

But again without permission, again in contempt of court, Hirschfeld removed lines from the 17 Park Avenue switchboard and workmen appeared at 15 Park Avenue to dismantle the passenger elevator to make it run automatically without an operator. Tenants were relegated to the service elevator which was badly in need of repair.

Several new tenants moved into the building. At least one of them had rented apartments in previous Hirschfeld-owned buildings before they became cooperatives. He openly

141

championed the landlord. We nicknamed him Houseplant.

Hirschfeld denied that he was converting the elevator though the workmen confirmed that he was. A tenant who was moving out claimed to have been refused the return of his security deposit unless he signed a letter supporting the changes. It didn't take us long to instigate a contempt proceeding against Hirschfeld before the New York Supreme Court.

♦

In the meantime, I was traveling a good deal with my job, mainly to Los Angeles for Toyota; Youngstown, Ohio, and Pittsburgh for Arby's, but I also wrote some freelance stories that involved short weekend trips.

My mother was calling me regularly because she wanted to go to England in the spring, and decided I should go with her. She would visit her mother's childhood home in Devon and spend time with numerous uncles and cousins but wanted company—and only her youngest daughter would suffice. I had not yet told her about David. As I wrote to him:

"I finally had to write my mother and tell her about you and the possibility that we might be married in the spring. I figured she'd get the letter Wednesday night, so I stayed out to 1:00 AM to avoid the phone. She called me at the office the next morning."

"It all sounds wonderful. He sounds wonderful."

"How are you, Mother?"

"Okay, except I couldn't sleep last night."

"So you must be tired."

"I just knew I'd burst into tears if anyone looked at me cross-eyed. And they did. And I did."

"What happened?"

"Can't you just figure out how to meet me in London?"

"Mother—that's why I wrote. To explain why I didn't know what I was doing."

"Well, can I show your brother and sister your letter?"

"If you must. What's new with you, Mother?"

"I trust your judgment."

"I'm not sure I trust my judgment."

"Well, I'm planning to go to Devon and then to visit Rosemary and Uncle Harry and Nora and can't you just spend one week with me?"

"Mother – the reason I wrote. . . ."

When David responded to my letter, he said: "Your mother sounds disturbed—and I don't mean upset."

♦

After my small red Fiat blew up, conveniently in front of a junk yard, Dad had lent me his second car, a Chevy Impala, for the summer. I'd garaged it in Tarrytown, considerably cheaper than in the city, and used it for the weekends. In mid-September I returned the Chevy for the winter.

I cornered my father as soon as I arrived at his house in Mathews.

"Listen, Dad, I have to tell you that I really care about David," I said. "But we only had a short time together in New York. I want to go visit him when I can. I think I love him a lot, but I need to be sure. And I need to be sure I can live in Lagos."

Dad wanted to know if David was good for me; then he wanted to know if David was good for me in bed. Good old Dad. I answered the first question in the affirmative; told him the second was none of his business, though he should have been able to guess the answer.

"I think you need to go," he said. "But I won't let anyone pay my daughter's expenses. You let me know the cost of the ticket, and I will send you the money." Yes, good old Dad!

The next week I obtained a passport and visited the Nigerian embassy for a visa application. There was hope.

Chapter Seventeen

He climbs
red dirt roads, rustles
red cloth doors. I know
his mouth, so bittersweet
it might be tasting truth.
Eyes that see
more than eyes
can see: barefoot boy, earthen pot,
banyon tree, the glimmer
of possibility, the afterglow.

From David: Sept 27, 1977
"I received two letters tonight from the reformed non-writer of letters and I am glad you finally got something from the African side.

"I like your letters; they're totally absurd and charming and nice to read over. Don't go too far toward changing things around in your head—or elsewhere. Just keep the faith and we'll work it all out soon. I love you, Sally, and only wish I could be there to tell you.

"I spent the weekend at Itu in Oko-Iboku— the site. It is most definitely in 'the jungle'—on the north side of the Cross River about one kilometer from a new bridge that will open this spring. Dirt roads, mud houses, thatched roofs, dugout canoes, monkeys chattering in the deeper forests, crocodile hunting in the swamps, and snakes of endless variety. Wild parrots and broadbills and eagles. Absolutely five hundred times better than Lagos.

"The site is not fully cleared, and work starts again the first of December. Hopefully housing will be up by mid-1979, and then mill construction will begin. I think the money for equipment will be released this week and the construction contract will be let October 10-15 at a board meeting. I hope. The contract will be the commitment that binds the Nigerians to going ahead with the project, and will signal the end to ten months of constipation.

"The French (Fougerolle) are building the Itu bridge and clearing our site, and I stayed in an eight-celled apartment in their expatriate camp. Most of the people are just returning from holidays; about ten families and six bachelors are in residence. The housing is pretty good, up high overlooking the river with completely self-contained electricity, water and PX. There is one tennis court, a dining hall with a bar and pool table and dart board. There are two movies a week, and swimming in the river during the dry season. The school takes care of some twenty-five children from five to twelve years of age. Not a paradise, but quite livable if you like poking around the countryside.

"Medical facilities are an hour and a half away by boat or three hours by car. At least five snake bites have been treated, two of which were fatal. One of the grass-cutting donkeys also died of a snake bite. There is no serum for the mamba, common in Nigeria.

"We took the Land Rover around the mill and town site which is very hilly and full of palm trees and Tarzan vines; we lost one Rover in the mud but finally pulled it loose with another Rover and fifteen locals at a payment of one naira per local.

"My driver and I took a two-hour ferry boat ride from Calabar downriver to Oron and then drove twelve hours over the worst roads (red line in Michelin) to get in about 1:30 this morning. The carnage along the roads is unbelievable. There were at least thirty accidents each way— flipped trucks, seven-vehicle get-togethers, bodies strewn everywhere. One stretch of road crosses twelve creeks in a hundred miles, and every crossing is by a one-lane bridge—no guard rails at the bottom of the hills—and every one had at least one car or truck in the river or lying along the right of way. No pavement in any of the towns along the way; no road maintenance, anywhere. Also no speed limit. We got stopped seven times by armed army types in camouflage suits on the way back—the car searched, papers checked—but there were no problems.

"In Lagos, in the fountain in the center of the banking district, a body floated face down all day. People selling peanuts and underwear and soap in little stalls and from trays on their heads did a better than average business.

"With a local banker, plus Hugh Calder and Forbes Peebles from the office in Croydon, I dined pool-side at the luxurious EKO Hotel.

Cocktails and a buffet were on the veranda overlooking the ocean. The beach is wide but separated from the hotel by barbed wire and chain link as several guests have evidently been stabbed and robbed by people living in villages on the beach.

"This is the far end of the beach; the other end, toward town, is where the public executions take place by firing squad.

"I will be looking for a house this week and next and will hopefully have something for the fifteenth of October for NNMC board approval. If the faint heartbeat of this project gets stronger by then I'll let Landegger know I will stay for a few more months at least and then, if you still want to, you can come over and see for yourself.

"I want you here right now, but it would be horrible in too many ways for you, as being in this house, in a slum between Lagos and the airport, is like being in prison. It's not safe to wander outside the house alone.

"Next day—and what a bomb. Hugh Calder, Forbes Peebles and I spent the day in the ministry finding out that the finance people don't want to process the documents returned to them by the Central Bank so no down payments on equipment contracts look possible for the next two months, which should blow off all the contracts made to date.

"Also, the Permanent Secretary of the Industrial Ministry has totally rejected the thirty-five million dollar construction contracts negotiated over the past three weeks and has demanded issuing tenders to more construction companies.

I believe that we face a twelve-month delay in the whole program—and no chance of any real savings.

"I would expect in the long run—if there is a long run—the project will see a thirty percent total cost increase.

"There is a budget meeting the tenth of October which should reflect this delayed timetable. By then I should know Landegger's reaction and know if I still have a job here and the go-ahead for housing more suitable for a lady visitor.

"I heard what you said about uncertainty, and I am trying my best to keep going in one direction that will bring us together soon, but these deflections are from way out there. I expect by the fifteenth or so to know. What is certain is that I love you, and we will get together, maybe back in NY, maybe here, before my visa is up the first week of December.

"Poor Calder goes back to London tonight dazed and discouraged at seeing six months of work go down the drain. He'll take this letter for posting. One bad thing is I won't hear from you for eleven days until the next group arrives from London.

"Don't give up on me, love. I wrote the kids the other day and told them I was planning to marry you and to get ready. I haven't had to worry about it for a long time, but finding the right lifestyle for us instead of just me is now consideration number one. I guess that's why all this pushing and pulling here seems less important. Nigeria may not be the best place to live, but it should be seen at least once. Grit your teeth (gently) for a little while and everything will be okay. We need to wait until this board meeting is over to figure out what is going on."

Chapter Eighteen

This refrain
my brain keeps
humming, a multitude
of messy tunes
searching for
true timbre.

Machetes and lethal violence, deadly snakes and fatal diseases, ubiquitous malaria, menacing corruption and crime. Countless car wrecks. Bodies floating in fountains. I had good reason to worry when I didn't hear from David over a period of time.

My friends found inventive ways to warn me about Nigeria. My former roommate and good friend Bonnie married a literary lawyer who gave me a book about the Lassa Fever epidemic which raged through Nigeria. Lassa Hemorrhagic Fever, a deadly disease carried by the Multimammate rat, was first identified in two mission nurses who were working in Lassa, the Jos region of Nigeria in 1969.

My boss told me outright that I should fall in love with someone else. I told him that Paul Newman was already married.

At the same time, New York wasn't getting any safer. That autumn a diamond dealer was robbed of $600,000 worth of gems, strangled and his body stuffed in a box in diamond cutter Shlomo Tal's office. Tal was eventually charged with the crime. And a few days after the diamond district killing, the cook at my neighborhood haunt, the Guardsman, was murdered. The city's violence had crept very close to home.

Despite what I was told, I was less concerned about living in West Africa than about whether or not David and I could sustain a long and satisfying relationship. I asked him to tell me about his fears, and sent him a long, tedious tape about my concerns.

I told him that I was used to being self-reliant; earning my own living, and was not sure I would feel comfortable being supported. I was fully ready to assume the compromises required for a successful relationship, but was concerned about the role I might be expected to play as a corporate wife, and how that role would mesh with my increasing desire to do more significant work.

"All the stuff I've said about this country," David wrote, "is not to scare you off. I'd like to have you here, and you'd enjoy the experience—for a while at least—because it is here. What I've been doing is purging my conscience. I want you to know what it's like—really how bad it could be for you, for me, for us. Lassa fever is no less fatal than the black or green mamba snake or the lynch mob two blocks from the office. I think about the dangers then climb back into the

152

leather cup with the other dumb dice and fall out at whatever odds prevail. That's okay for me to do, but I don't think it's okay for me to do to thee. It is equally unfair for me to not let you decide.

"I want you here, but I want you knowledgeable and reasonably safe. I have sent Landegger a message asking to see him in London or Paris within the next three weeks. I want to tell him in person my assessment about the project, and I want to tell him about us and under what terms I can stay here with you. Otherwise, I want another assignment. That's not your fault or responsibility; it's mine.

"I promise you I won't be unemployed on the day we get married. (Maybe promise is too strong a word). I love you and, for me, there hasn't been anybody like you in my whole life. And I need whatever you are.

"In the next fifty years or so we can move on to the really important matter of how two people, independently set in their ways, survive the compromises required to become an amicable couple. If we really enjoy each other, these inevitable adjustments will happen because that's how we get what we want—each other. And if we really respect each other's individuality—which is what attracts one to the other, then neither tries to mold or style the other.

"There is no reason to rush into marriage until you feel comfortable about doing so. I feel comfortable now, but I'll feel just as comfortable a year from now if you need more time. So relax a little.

"I fully expect you and me to keep on growing and changing and seeking new ways to obtain self-satisfaction, and it would be disastrous if that didn't happen. One might as well form an enduring relationship with a plastic plant.

"I am glad you are going through all the serious thought processes, because it is serious. I don't have all the answers; I just have infinite love for you and maybe most of the answers will come from that. Just be patient a bit longer. I love you.

"And I need you to help me climb back into the world.

"PS. This letter is turning into a two-pound term paper."

◆

The decrepit service elevator in 15 Park Avenue went out for four hours while the new self-service passenger elevator was still being installed. The tenants were enraged. Even so, as promised, I held a meeting to present the new lobby plans. The meeting lasted two hours, and the tenants (except for Houseplant) refused to accept the new plans. Harold invited me to his apartment for a stiff drink. I readily accepted. I was exhausted, and when I returned to my apartment, Hirschfeld's decorator called asking what color rugs I preferred for the new lobby. I told him that there was no new lobby that I knew of.

The next phone call was from a *Village Voice* reporter. As soon as I mentioned Hirschfeld, there was a loud click and the phone went dead.

He called back. I mentioned Houseplant by name. There was another click. Assuming that my phone was tapped, we made a lunch appointment for an interview.

I heard next from a tenant in a West Side building which Hirschfeld had purchased then began converting to a cooperative. "When I objected," she said, "Hirschfeld called me a prostitute. I was so angry I hired a lawyer and went to court against him."

She said that, while she was stating her case in court, Houseplant, who then lived in her building, nailed her door shut.

Just after I arrived at the office the next morning I heard from our landlord. "We should work together," he said. "Otherwise you'll lose. We've been opposed by lawyers who are lots tougher than yours, and we've always won."

That afternoon there was a call from the rent commission insisting on a Thursday hearing on the lobby change. Was it payoff time?

It was becoming obvious that we were dealing with a man who would use tough tactics to get what he wanted. For now I had the full support of Harold and Lou and an army of righteously angry tenants behind me and saw no reason to give in.

Despite it being a workday afternoon, that Thursday thirty tenants gathered in the rotunda of the Supreme Court building and sat as a group at the hearing. The judge loudly and clearly indicated his displeasure at Hirschfeld beginning work on the 15 Park Avenue elevator while under a work-stoppage court order. He again ordered the work stopped. We requested that it not be stopped since, in the meantime, the tenants of that building had to use the unreliable service elevator.

Hirschfeld was granted a one-week adjournment to get papers together on the third term of our suit, where we asked for $6,000 a day while the passenger elevator was out of service.

Early in the morning on the nineteenth of October, the phone rang. I'd had enough calls that week regarding the building, so I snuggled down into my bed and was about to cover my face—or, better yet, the phone—with my pillow when I decided to answer it. David was calling from Nigeria. His voice was low and sensual. He said hello and gently laughed. I hugged the phone to my ear and asked him to laugh again.

That afternoon I wrote: "Guess who woke me up this morning—and did I ever love it! It was incredibly good to talk to you, but you know the best part? Hearing you laugh! You can't laugh in a letter or even in a tape without it sounding strange—but did it ever turn me on!

"You sounded good. I love you. If you don't set up a meeting with Landegger at some place I can get to in the next month, and it looks as if you are there for the long term, then I can start to plan a trip there for the end of November, even if you are still living in the prison. Otherwise we'll make some plans for December—somewhere and somehow. They have to let you out of there *sometime*!

"I just wanted you to know that you can wake me up anytime. I am okay, only frustrated that I can't show you that I love you every day.

"P.S. Do Lagos newspapers report such world-important events such as the fact that Reggie Jackson hit three home runs last night to win the series for the Yankees?"

♦

Not wanting to face another unpredictable Virginia winter, David's parents sold Oakland Farm and moved to Florida. When Dad told me Tony and Phoebe would be back in Mathews County for a friend's mid-October wedding, he also said I shouldn't bother coming down. I booked a flight immediately. The Monday after my trip to Mathews I wrote to David:

"And all along you thought I loved you. Nope. It's your parents I love. Maybe I love you because I love your parents, or maybe I love your parents because I love you. Or maybe I love you and your parents, though not exactly in the same way.

"Getting to see them was like getting close to you for a couple of hours. They looked healthy, happy and, well, just sparkling! A lot of that was because they had just seen your girls and were so pleased with them. Your mom kept saying 'they're great kids!' They must be great kids— just look at their father (and don't I just wish I could)!

"I kept getting the feeling that your parents love you very much and care about you, but in a

157

non-possessive way. How did you do that? Can I adopt your parents, please?

"David, here's what I want to do.

"I want to touch you, kiss you, be hugged by you, have breakfast with you, lunch with you, dinner with you, take a long walk with you, listen when you're happy, listen when you're unhappy, accept the fact that you love me, even if you're acting as if you don't.

"I want to surprise you, sail with you, love what you love, celebrate with you when good things happen, wake up with you beside me, look at giraffes with you, let you know when I'm mad at you, take pictures together, clean the lint from your navel, put my head on your chest, give you the freedom to be, let you go when you need to go, accept you when you want to stay.

"I want to hear leaves crunch under your feet, watch your footsteps form in the sand, respect you even when I think you're wrong, feel the sweaty back of your neck, laugh at something you said, remain excited over who you are, tell you that you're weird, tell you that you're funny, hear you tell me how much you care, go flying with you, go flying without you and know it's okay, go to a toy store together, go to a museum together, a grocery store, go home together, feel free to be myself with you, love you when you're unlovable, love you when I don't feel like loving anyone at all.

"I want to have you keep me warm, look at new places with you, go back to old places with you, give up something for you, accept something from you, share a memory with you, share an adventure, be apart while we're together, plant a garden with you, tell you when I'm afraid, tell you when I'm depressed.

"I want to tell you that I love you, love a puppy with you, a child, your children.

"I want to have you cook me breakfast, cook breakfast for you, wash (but never iron) your clothes, play you a game of darts, make you smile, make you laugh, make you happy, read what you read, talk about it.

"I want to sit by a fire with you, have a snowball fight with you, ski with you, take a shower with you, cook a Thanksgiving dinner together, trim a Christmas tree, make a dream come true with you, accept a dream that failed with you, do something I don't want to do for you, refuse to do something you want me to do if I really don't want to do it, have you tell me you're unhappy with something I said or did. Grow with you. Change with you. Look at you. Talk to you. Live with you. Share with you. Be with you. Love you. And that's all I want to do— except win the Nobel Prize.

"What's going on over there???? Hello?"

Chapter Nineteen

In a life
of so many
starts,
pauses;
so many possibilities
recklessly ignited
and slowly smothered,
isn't it amazing
I still believe

if
once more
I rub
the magic lamp
a genie
may actually appear.

David, November 2, 1977
"Do you realize that I have been here for sixty days, and it seems like sixty years and that it is your fault? I am now one hundred and one years old.

"Are you aware that I haven't written you in a long time because I didn't want to tell you all the depressing, confidence-eroding, stupid and frustrating things that have been happening here? I did cut a depressing tape finally but Nigeria Airways crashed a 707 on the runway and there wasn't any airmail, but now there is so I'll send it, though things aren't quite so bad.

"Today we got the money for the equipment approved. Today we got the letters of credit. Today we got the funding for NNMC for 28 million Naira and they have agreed to pay the overdue PWL invoices tomorrow. Today was a pretty damn good day! Monday Jim Hayes, the new managing director of PWL, comes to Lagos. Timing is all.

"There is a spider in this typewriter. Do they get headaches? If you were here, we could go on a celebratory drunk with the spider and all get headaches, but since you're not, we won't. We can wait a little longer. A LITTLE longer.

"Summer is beginning here. From now through February there should be almost no rain; a dry, hazy atmosphere should prevail. The days are getting shorter while the sun is getting stronger. I am boggled. The exodus to Mecca is in full swing with a purported hundred thousand Nigerians flying to Saudi Arabia. Christmas cards have made their way into the stores, and strings of lights for your banana tree are everywhere. An anonymous person dropped a neatly-wrapped corpse at the post office. No return address. Zone three, Lagos, accounts for 2,312 pails of night soil per night. No figures for zone one or two.

"And that's enough shit for that paragraph.

"Ray Charles is singing Porgy and Bess on Voice of America, and your letter just arrived. He shouldn't sing Porgy and Bess. You should write more lists. That's beautiful. You're beautiful. You sure make it easy for this man to love you. If I act as if I don't it's for your own good. And it's only an act."

◆

Sally, November 2, 1977 Night Letter
"No mail concerns me. You okay?   In Ohio Thursday, Atlanta Friday night through Tuesday AM. Can you telex 7105815087 DFS or cable DAFISAM? I'll get the message. I love you."

◆

Sally, November 2, 1977
"I just sent you message via whatever since there were no telex or cable listings. The last mail predated our phone conversation, and I was about to leave town which would mean no access to the maddening mailbox for a least five more days. I have to run off to Josh's to sign an affidavit, then go home and pack. Hello out there, and I love you!"

◆

David, November 4, 1977 Telex
"Not to worry. Recent depression succumbs to current high. Boeing in Bush mired mail. But letter and tape in transit. Have named ulcer Latunde as Peter Principle assumes epidemic proportions and national prominence. Cash crunch crisis causing caustic criticism concerning contract continuing, however, the crisis

163

is in hand. Your feelings reciprocated with undiminished enthusiasm.

"Say hi to your mom."

◆

Sally, November 4, 1977
"In transit, Youngstown, Ohio to Atlanta. I just had a ten minute stop in Akron which gave me time to call the office, and my secretary relayed what little she understood of your cable. In the meantime, knowing you are okay makes everything okay here. Thank you for your rapid response. Karen did get the part across that mail was forthcoming, so I will look forward to returning to NYC even more than I usually would.

"Youngstown. The new Arby's are the highlight of the city, not to mention the best places to eat. More steel shutdowns, more unemployment, fewer people, no money, no fun. But, also no traffic, which was good since I had to cover five Arby's and check promotions in at least twenty-five discount stores in half a day."

◆

My first night in Atlanta, my mother and I had dinner with Kitty and Elliott Galloway and their sons, Jeff and Charlie. Mother had worked for Elliott when he was middle-school principal of The Westminster Schools; their son, Jeff, had competed in the 1972 Olympic Games, and was

164

emerging as an authority on long-distance running.

The son of a cotton and tobacco farmer from Moultrie, Georgia, Elliott Galloway resolutely plowed his way into Wake Forest College then harvested success after success, first as a Commander in the Navy and then as an educator. In 1969, Elliott founded the progressive, nongraded Galloway School by converting a condemned Chastain Park almshouse built in 1911 into classrooms.

Elliott Galloway was a philosopher who eagerly quoted John Dewey and Paul Tillich; a mathematician; a theologian who had completed two years of study at Columbia and Union Theological Seminary in New York; a highly-respected and charismatic headmaster who felt that education should evoke in children a life-long love of learning.

When other independent schools in the South were building enrollments based on the fear of integration, Dexter and Martin Luther King III were welcomed as students at The Galloway School.

Elliott Galloway was the godfather to one of my nieces, and his office desk had once been my grandfather's. He advised and counseled many Atlanta youngsters, including me, urging us to risk failure in an attempt to succeed and to continue to learn and grow after becoming adults.

After dinner that night, Elliott drew me aside in the living room, removed stacks of books from two chairs, sat down and displayed the hypnotic smile that revealed the space between his two front teeth. His voice was Southern, soft, like drawing a shoe across fine sand. He asked, as he always did, "How are you coming along with your work?"

He meant my life's work—all aspects—not just what I did for a living. He leaned back in his chair and chewed on the left temple of his glasses.

"My job is good; the agency is a great place to work. When we lost the Bayer account, nobody was fired; they were put to work on new business, and brought in Hunt's."

"Is that right?"

I nodded. "I'm enjoying tutoring my student, Timmy. I love the one-on-one, urging him forward at his own pace. I learned that from you." Elliott smiled.

"Because of my landlord, we're in court a lot. But the tenants are determined, and we're winning the fight. It's important to our elderly residents. I'm learning about the legal system."

Elliott then folded his glasses and put them down on the stack of books beside him. "I'd like you to help me put together some brochures to go after a potential endowment," he said. "Someday we also need to work together on a book about the school."

"I can't make any promises now," I said. "David is still trying to sort out his job and a way for us to be together. All I really want is to be with him. We haven't had much time, but we both have been open with each other, and I am feeling comfortable with our relationship." I chuckled. "If you can actually have a relationship

166

with someone who lives seven thousand miles away."

"It's possible that you won't be married," he said.

His remark startled me. I shrugged, then shook my head. "But I love him more than I have ever loved anyone," I replied—as if love were all that was needed.

And I realized for the first time, perhaps, how very much I really did want to marry David.

♦

"Sally, continued November 7:
Atlanta: three Arby's, one Grand National stock car race for STP and twelve discount stores later. America is in deep trouble. Giant K-Marts and Woolcos and Richways and Zayres taking over the country, and all jammed with junk America can't live without: hamburger machines, hair machines, machine machines, leisure suits, Ex-lax, STP, Evil Knievel toys—and I saw it all, store after store, and kept thinking that it would be nice to be somewhere where you couldn't buy anything. How's this for a great disaster movie: A giant K-Mart keeps growing. Oh, I guess it's already been done, and in real vision.

"The track was wet most of the day with rain, so all but about 25 laps were run under the yellow flag with no position changes. STP does a great job of visibility, and Richard Petty is as good a spokesperson who ever came out of the back woods of North Carolina, but the real experience is in the infield, gaping at the gaping spectators in their enormous motor homes plastered with pictures of Cale Yarborough, Richard Petty, Bobby Allison or Buddy Baker, and all wearing T-shirts, jackets, hats and (I assume) undershorts advertising their favorite driver. Drinking beer, bellies hanging out over those shorts, listening to the race on plastic transistor radios purchased at K-Mart. It doesn't take much to satisfy Americans, I guess—and they sure looked satisfied.

"It doesn't take much to satisfy me, either—just David Stiles. And the Nobel Prize. Both are in the same class and both very far away."

"I don't think I want to wait to get married. I want to be with you more than I want to do anything else. I am as sure as I will ever be, and I love you immensely. I need you, and you are all I need. I WANT A DATE AND A PLACE!!!

"If you really want me, you've got me. For better or worse for either of us. So let's do it.

"PS. I just got in to discover still no mail. Three weeks now. Forget the wedding. I think I'll kill myself. Or you. Or the Nigerian postal service. Is there such a thing?

♦

David, November 6, 1977
"It must be at least the twenty-fifth day without electricity, and all that goes with it. I am typing by candle light to keep the sweat from making the paper too wet to take ink, avoiding the gas lantern that raises the temperature another fifty degrees. I am trying to decide whether reading by

candlelight is better or worse than going to bed at 8:00. As I look up from the keyboard, I am disappointed at not seeing Sidney Greenstreet lounging in the chair opposite. By mounting one candle on the left side of the carriage and another on the right side it is almost possible to type in the dark.

"I scooped a foot-long lizard out of the toilet last night; it seemed to appreciate its freedom, but the chickens got him before he made it to the bush.

"I went to Mathew Mbu's house this morning with Peter driving like he was entering the last lap of the Indy 500 with a six-inch lead. There was a 9:00 AM execution of six men at Bar Beach, so he dropped me off and returned to report: 'Yasssuh, they went off right at the time. One man he die very hard, suh. They shoot him and his head come back up. They shoot him again but he not yet dead. Many people there, shouting and clapping hands to shoot him again. They shoot him one more time and he die at that moment.'

"Whether you are crazy or not seems hardly significant at this point. What you are is what you are, is what I want and love and need. So I'm crazy, too, and that's good because you want and need and love me and, if one of us becomes sane, will the other one know whose hand is being held?

"The next time we meet need not be in an airport chapel. We can and do have the time we need to be calm and sure, if that is the problem. Life is about enjoying, accepting, expanding, exploring, risking, hoping, failing, feeling, trying, winning, giving, doing, loving and it's all living and you just do the best you can with it. I forgot to add pontificating.

"If I were a Nigerian trying to work out a government contract in Washington would it be any easier? I don't think so. I so seldom see other white men that it comes as a surprise sometimes that I have white skin.

"Ah! The electricity just came on! I'm blind!! Ice cubes tomorrow.

"You must choose: Abe wants to break both your legs, and I want to make love to you for the rest of your life. There are other options, but we can ignore them as this is a setup, so only two options are on the ballot. The first option would require my involvement, as I would reciprocate and would probably end up incarcerated. The second option I can't count on since I have never made love to *me*, and it could be worse than two broken legs.

"Due to an audible explosion outside we are again corresponding by candlelight. Or not. Goodnight for now.

"And good morning! How did these mountains of wax get all over everything?

"The mill project is, at the moment, going very well. My Nigerian associates are more relaxed, cooperative and trusting. There will continue to be problems and sizeable delays, but eventually rolls of newsprint will come stumbling out of the jungle. Eighteen months or so before that happens, another managing director will take over here, but there is another mill in the

Sudan which is at about the same state of development as this one, and by then it may need my attention. In the meantime, I believe I will be here, and it would be good if you could come so we could look at it together and decide if we really want to start a life here or whether we would be better off trying elsewhere. You have every right to be in the right place for you.

"We could meet in London or Spain or someplace and have a wonderful and unreal holiday, but I would rather we had a real living experience which would either preserve or eliminate an option. I am not going anyplace unless you tell me you aren't coming here. Then I'll come to you. I'd have to. You are it, and I will never get over the feeling of pure pleasure that revelation brings. I savor it every day and have built the rest of my life around it; around you and us. We are the only ones who know how it is between us, and what we are now. Nobody else has experienced us. Come soon."

♦

Sally, November 10, 1977
"It's about midnight and I'm really tired, except that I've been thinking of you for the last eight hours and I guess the only sensible thing for me to do is get something about what's going on inside of me down on paper. This may be a confusing letter since my feelings are flowing rather quickly and are scrambled.

"Except for the cable, it's been since the 19th of October—the day you called—that I have

171

received any news from you. I can't go for almost a month without hearing from you.

"I think of the some eleven letters I've sent into the West African void and think, well, here goes another one. (I hope you're not paying me back for not writing when you were in Algeria.)

"I need to know that you're okay and that you still love me. It's not your fault that I let you turn my life around. . . .

"Maybe we should think in terms of: perhaps it will work a year from now. That way we can both calm down and let what happens happen in the meantime. I am not writing this to hurt you. I'm not trying to manipulate you. I am just trying to explain that I'm terribly unhappy with the way things are, and I think we need a new approach."

◆

Sally, November 12, 1977 Sweepstakes

ANNOUNCING THE
YOU ASKED FOR IT, YOU GOT IT
SWEEPSTAKES

ENTER TODAY TO WIN AN INCREDIBLE
ONE OF A KIND PRIZE!

GRAND PRIZE:
All five-foot-four inches of woman, willing and able to love and cherish you! Entertaining, considerate, warm. Experienced private pilot, author. Foremost expert on snowmobiles and

172

Arby's roast beef sandwiches. Able to stand up to bad landlords. Teeth fixed. Educated and analyzed. Can withstand extremes of climate and amenities. Comes complete with barber chair and small library. Must be seen to be believed!

OFFICIAL RULES:

Complete the following questionnaire by checking one category only. Response must be received by November 24, 1977 to be eligible to win. Telephone call makes for instant winner if received by deadline.

Sweepstakes is open only to employees of Parsons & Whittemore in Lagos, Nigeria who are 41 years of age, hold official U.S. passports and have handsome if largish ears.

No purchase required. Only one prize will be awarded. Prize is not taxable.

OFFICIAL ENTRY FORM
PLEASE INDICATE YOUR CHOICE CLEARLY.

_____A. Your prize is currently holding reservations to arrive in Lagos on December 17 with a return reservation on January 2. Checking this category means that you wish her to pick up her tickets by November 25, 1977. *Bonus Prize for This Category*: She will bring plum pudding for Christmas.

_____B. Category A is not feasible at this time, however you wish to see her as soon as possible. *Note: To win this category, you must indicate where and when.*

_____C. She should hold off. You've got other plans, or hope to have other plans.

173

♦

David, November 13, 1977

"My London colleagues just left. I had more
incoming mail from you this week than any other
and no time to answer until now as I was
occupied with the new Managing Director of
PWL. Jim Hayes is a very nice man with much
foreign experience and a refreshing American 'get
the job done' approach.

"Instead of being the summer replacement
resident liaison officer, I am now the Managing
Director of the Nigerian Newsprint Manufac-
turing Company which means I can get on with
it. I now have the authority to form this company
and run it as I think it should be run. I have
worked out a staff requirement for thirty people
for the next six months.

"Your last letter took a surprising turn. You
love my parents and are beginning to organize a
wedding. Terrific!!! I'm ready. Take me, you fool!
I told Jim about it in case it changed his plans
for me here, and there is no problem. He was
concerned as to whether or not you'd live here.
Me, too. But I think you will end up liking it.

"I really considered coming home the other
night. Between the mail, the photographs you
sent and being in the airport when the Pan Am
flight arrived from New York via Accra, the need
to be with you took me by the hand, and I was
willing to be led.

"I want to tell you again that I have no
intention of ever going anywhere or doing

anything that keeps us apart. This has been a proving experience, and the sooner it ends, the better.

"You asked about the children. Divorcing children is a dangerous game as you well know. I tried to prepare them and me for the results, but the first year was a bitch. After some hesitation, the children began to respond to me as I had hoped—not for my sake as much as for theirs. Sometimes the distinction gets lost. That leaves about nine million words which you are welcome to hear at any time, but not through the mail. On the whole they are very neat people going through the growing up process as individuals: strength through adversity, I hope . . . .

"They have two reservations about our getting married. First, they wonder if you haven't picked an old man. 'From what I understand gusto runs out after a certain age.' And they want to know where and when so they can 'drop in'. I would really have to stretch my imagination to imagine them not liking you, or you not liking them. Hell, I'm stuck with all of you—and loving it.

"In spite of your running off on long week-ends with Richard Petty, you remain the meaning in my life, and I love you more than I can begin to tell you."

◆

Sally, November 14, 1977 RCA Night Letter
"In case you could use company for Xmas, have booked Pan Am arriving Lagos Dec 17, returning

January 2. This may seem confusing in light of letters of Nov 8 and 10, but explained in Nov 14 letter. What a way to run a relationship! Need response by Nov 25 to get ticket. Love, Sally

◆

Sally, November 14, 1977
"Last week I sent you three letters, each going off into a different direction. I sent one letter saying I wanted to see you, marry you right away and the next one saying let's forget this entirely, and a third which gave you a chance to win me for Christmas. I doubt if you are as confused by them as you should be since you possess a greater-than-average share of intelligence and must, by now, be used to my waffling. Continued lack of mail from Lagos means no new input as to your plans and means that I am carrying on a one-way communication which seldom makes much sense.

"You didn't, by any chance, send that promised letter and tape through Croydon to be shipped back by boat and held up by the current dock strike, did you?

◆

David, November 14, 1977
"You're creating a paper shortage! Congratulations!

"I spent my first day as Managing Director of NNMC establishing personnel policies to fit government guidelines, looking at office space and housing for us and the Croydon transients on Victoria Island.

"While everything takes ten times longer to do here than anywhere else I have ever been, I hope to have this real estate BS put aside by the first week in December.

"Your reaction to gluttonous purchasing in the US was the same as mine after the Algerian adventure. People don't need all that shit. Horror movie #4: An explosion in a chemical plant in San Jose sends a huge cloud of toluene across the country, melting all plastic in its path, and everything slumps into grotesque piles; the warehouse wall at Zayres bursts open, sending a terrorizing torrent of gray-green glop out to swallow the camera and then the audience before disappearing into the oily sea.
"I LOVE YOU, TOO, SO STOP SHOUTING!!!
Iloveyouverymuchhewhisperedsoftlyacross seventhousandmilesofoceananduptheeastriver."

♦

David, November 15, 1977
"Neither of my guests from London could get on the plane for Calabar this morning, so Peter took them off to town. I drove—without incident or license—to the architect's office and then to NET to call you, but the phone line was out to the street. I also wanted to send a telex to London but the telex line was out to the street so I rotated by the super market. Wow! My favorite toothpaste was for sale there, even with a free toothbrush inside. Vodka was on the shelf for the

first (and probably only) time. A recognizable (Haig Pinch) brand of Scotch was right there, as were bags of frozen shrimp. A fantastic day! A day without equal!

"Are you really going to be here in 32 days? I think I will write a nice letter to Mr. Tugbobo at the Ministry of Industries and let him know how happy I am. He's never seen me smile."

♦

David, November 16, 1977
"Hello sweet Sally—your tape arrived today, one month old—good, good, terrific! I will put a loving you response in the mail tomorrow. There's not much to say of importance, but lots to resay. When you get here in December you'll be in very deep trouble as I have friends in high places to help in the kidnapping."

♦

Sally, November 16, 1977
"Happy Thanksgiving. You may not have a surfeit of cranberry sauce available and capturing one of those street turkeys may be tricky; conjuring up something to be thankful for may also be a problem, but, at least, I am sure you can make it all up in yams.

"If you converted the site into a yam patch, then converted yams into the national currency or, better yet, figure out how to convert yams into petroleum, I think all your problems would be solved."

◆

Sally November 18, 1977
"I received your long, typed letter last night and all of a sudden everything seemed to fall into place with the realization that I might actually see you again after all. I am a new person or, perhaps, my old person again. I like the way you like lists. . . .

"I think that one of the reasons I thought you and I would never work out is that nothing as good as us has ever happened in the world before."

◆

Sally, November 21, 1977
"This morning I heard you laugh again, and I have to tell you that's one beautiful sound!

"I am feeling more than totally happy, and all that happiness belongs to you.

"Your horoscope in today's paper said 'you should contact somebody who cares about you.' I am glad it was me you called instead of Landegger."

◆

David, November 22, 1977
"Some eight men got into a loud and violent fight in front of the house Sunday over a minor car accident. One of them started swinging a steel rod at the others—so I stepped out onto the balcony and they stopped fighting with each

179

other to yell at me. Fortunately the only shit that came over the fence at me was verbal.

"Monday I took my steward, Umaru, and his children, to join some thousand Muslims at a prayer ground next to a turkey farm. Very friendly, colorful and some good pictures of the event. Also the quickest ceremony I've ever attended. The big guy gets up, everyone bows twice and breaks for the highway while he's still reading. A twelve-year-old boy tried to sell me his little brother, and I was tempted as he had big ears and would have fit into the family circle easily enough.

"The biggest news is that the electricity stayed on for twenty-six hours in a row starting Sunday night at 10:35, Allah be praised, all praise be to Allah. Maybe that will stop people from calling NEPA (Nigerian Electric Power Company) the No Electric Power Again Company. And I can finally say see you soon!"

♦

Sally, November 26, 1977
"I'll be seeing you and touching you and loving you in person in only 20 days, depending on the fates, Pan Am and the whim of the consulate at 575 Lexington Avenue.

"I just finished reading an Updike novel, the last of 27,000,000 novels over the past 1,000 years or so in which affairs are more interesting than marriages. Why? Maybe someday I will write the world's first novel about a good marriage. But I'll have to experience it first.

I managed to survive unruffled my first three and a half hours of Nigerian bureaucracy, going back to the window four times. The form I received two weeks ago and had filled out was, of course, no longer the correct form, so I had to complete the new six-page form in triplicate. It wasn't enough to say no, I had not served in the military, but also explain that I hadn't been in the army, air force, navy or marines and had not received a rank at discharge. Stuff like that. And then the matter of not having $2.30 exact change. But at least I got to the 'call back Tuesday' stage.

"I returned from Life Extension in the blowing rain, my arms full of shots. The direct flight on Pan Am is still up in the air, though I do now have first priority and should know Tuesday. I am still booked on the Monrovia junket and on a KLM through Amsterdam though that flight involves a 15% surcharge for my four-hour European holiday in the Amsterdam airport.

"My student, Timmy, is depressed as hell that I am going away for a few weeks. Poor Timmy. I feel so guilty about leaving him that I've been giving him homework assignments that don't quit, trying to teach him everything I know in the next two weeks. I don't know much, but he doesn't know anything at all. At least I have convinced him that he is not dying. Perhaps it's the nutrition lesson I gave him; maybe it's

181

because he is still alive. Last night I discovered I still had some serious work to do.

"*Sally:* 'Timmy, what did Leonardo DaVinci paint?'

"*Timmy:* 'The Mona Lisa.'

"*Sally:* 'That's terrific, Timmy! How did you know that?'

"*Timmy:* 'I guessed.'

"*Sally:* 'What else made DaVinci famous?'

"*Timmy:* 'He painted Winston Churchill.'

"*Sally:* 'Tim, Who was Winston Churchill?'

"*Timmy:* 'A general in the Marines.'

"*Sally:* 'Why do think Winston Churchill was a general in the Marines?'

"*Timmy:* 'I seen his picture in a jeep with a big cigar, you know? So he couldn't have been in the Air Force or the Navy. He must have been in the Marines.'

"I love you, David. I love you today more than yesterday, and yesterday I loved you more than the day before.

"Dad told me to get married in Lagos if I wanted to. My mother keeps trying to send me golf skirts and suitcase dividers. I am not sure she has totally processed where I am going."

◆

David, November 26, 1977
(the letter is carefully burned around the edges)
"I DON'T WANT TO START OUT SHOUTING, BUT there is no electricity for the four thousandth time. The replacement car broke down on the way to Lagos this morning. There was no

personal mail from Croydon this week. I spent three and a half hours at NET to get a busy signal. I threw three consecutive darts off the board this afternoon.

"ON THE OTHER HAND, I love you so much that everything else is irrelevant. Maybe for Christmas you could bring a good paperback dictionary."

♦

Sally, November 27, 1977
"Dear Managing Director:

"I just received your three letters of the 18th and I LOVE YOU!!!

"I wonder how it will feel not missing you anymore. Maybe I'll hate it.

"The Salvation Army is on the streets, and Lord & Taylor is putting up their Christmas windows, and there is a tree being decorated at Rockefeller Center.

"Don't tell me that I love you more than I love Christmas in New York! How the hell did that happen?"

♦

Sally, November 28, 1977
"You needn't be jealous of Richard Petty because, as you can see from this picture, we were well chaperoned. I'm giving up all this for some guy with big ears who lives in the Yam Capitol of the world? Please explain:

_____

_____."

♦

Sally, November 30, 1977
"Dear Instant Winner:

"Congratulations, and I do hope you will be pleased with your prize. Oh, how I hope.

"It's about 6:15 at the office now. There I was, innocently trying to concentrate on Toyota, then Arby's. The Arby's Currier & Ives glasses are, by the way, breaking all sales records. Work is becoming somewhat frantic as I try to clear off my desk between visits to the consulate. But it will get done . . . if I remove your picture from my desk.

"Another go-around with Pan Am today resulted in a ticket via Amsterdam on KLM. I now leave the evening of the 15th and arrive in Lagos at 5:45 PM on the 16th, Allah willing. Heh, heh, one whole day sooner. 'It wasn't my fault, Boss, the plane was all booked.' Unfortunately I won't be able to claim anymore that I have never been to Europe. . . .

"I had another visit to the consulate today which resulted in nothing. I have yet in my visits there to see anyone leave with a visa."

♦

Sally, December 4, 1977
"You sounded understandably tired and unbelievably grumpy on the phone when you called from London yesterday. I am sorry the mail took so long reaching you but, hopefully,

there will be letters and tapes waiting when you return to Lagos. I did not neglect you.

"You don't have to like Christmas, but I intend to be fully happy this Christmas because I am in love and will be with the man I love. I can't make up for your Christmases past, nor will I expect you to make up for mine. I can't fill all the voids, and neither can you. But this Christmas is a new beginning for both of us, and I intend to make the most of it.

"I will be seeing you soon and how nice that will be. This is absolutely the last time I will write I LOVE YOU on a machine until I can see you and say it in person and talk to you and hug you and enjoy every minute of being with you every single day."

Chapter Twenty

☆
One
palm frond
wedged into
a blue mop bucket;
two tin soldiers; three
Christmas cards; six
candy canes; popcorn strung
between twelve Portuguese
trade beads, and an over-the-top
tinfoil star. Woman. Man.
Comfort. And
so much
joy.

The KLM flight touched down at 6:30 in the evening. I leapt out of my seat and pressed my way off the plane onto a tarmac scorching from a day of Lagos heat. Air warmer and heavier than any dog day afternoon I remembered from my childhood in Georgia smote me, enveloped me, slowed my New York City stride. I removed my jacket, smoothed the wrinkles from my skirt and strolled to the immigration desk, already simulating a leisurely and assured African pace.

And as I walked toward the low-slung partially-roofed building, there arose the faint trace of an odor which I had not smelled since I was a child in Japan. It came back to me immediately: the acrid, sour, permeating stench of open sewers.

What I didn't want was to anger a Nigerian official; what I definitely didn't want was to be taken into custody in West Africa. I knew enough to be patient, respectful and, if possible, charming. The lines were long, disjointed, with people constantly shuffling from one place to another; I felt the surge of anxious individuals all around me. Finally it was my turn.

"What is the purpose of your visit?" The black man in a green uniform spoke in a clipped and lilting British/Nigerian accent while holding his stamp above my passport.

I smiled broadly. "I am here to visit my fiancé for Christmas."

He frowned. "Is he Nigerian?"

I wondered what the right answer was, but knew better than to guess.

"No sir," I said. "He is American. He is working here."

I was worried that I had given the wrong answer. The agent put his stamp down and flipped through my passport then carefully examined the tourist visa it had taken me weeks of patient pleading to obtain from the Nigerian consulate in New York.

"This is your first visit to Nigeria?"

Despite the oppressive heat, the swarm of insistent, fidgeting bodies around me, I smiled again. "It is. I am so happy to finally have a chance to experience your country."

"Na so?" Now his face broke into a huge grin, a mouthful of large teeth radiating. He pounded his stamp onto my passport, flipped through my new and uncreased yellow immunization book which confirmed recent shots for cholera, typhoid, paratyphoid, smallpox and yellow fever. "Enjoy your visit," he said. "Next?"

I edged a few paces forward and waited while an official argued loudly with a heavy Nigerian woman who finally reached into her orange printed dress and withdrew a dingy banknote. She crumpled it with one hand and slid it across the counter. The official laid his hand over hers and said "dis 'ting be guud."

Without even looking up at me, he stamped my declaration for the two hundred dollars in traveler's checks and fifty-seven U.S. dollars, thirty seven cents in my possession.

I'd faced two Nigerian officials and had not yet paid any *dash*. I was feeling pretty proud of myself.

But I still had to go through customs. I'd once had cameras confiscated entering Canada on a magazine assignment, so had packed my camera, a zoom lens and some twenty rolls of film in my suitcase to make them less apparent.

But as I approached the customs desk, a young Nigerian wearing a bright turquoise short-sleeve shirt and faintly pink pants approached me.

"I am Tunji," he said. "I am an employee of Mr. Stiles." He pointed beyond the desk and there, just behind the window grates and a waist-high concrete barrier, was David, wearing a button-down blue Oxford shirt. He looked thin, worried, and was turned toward a shorter, even thinner young black man beside him. I surmised that the younger man was Peter, David's driver.

Just then David and the young man beside him both laughed, and David looked up, peered over the barrier, saw me, and his face relaxed into a quiet smile. He nodded and spoke to Peter whose face scanned the customs area with wide-eyed curiosity.

I realized that Tunji was the tout David said might help me through the airport. Still, I hadn't expected to see him inside the customs area.

Tunji picked up my suitcase and placed it on the customs bench, spoke very quickly to the officer, slapped his hand and nodded at me. I looked at the stern, robust man in uniform, waiting for him to ask me what I had to declare, then to open my bag for inspection.

"Have you brought any gifts?" he asked in a deep, thunderous voice.

"I only have some books—and this bottle of Scotch." I held up the duty-free bag.

He looked with some degree of longing at the bag holding the bottle. At that moment, I would have willingly given it up to be allowed to pass through and get to David. But the officer simply nodded—first at Tunji then at me. "Welcome to Nigeria," he said. I smiled, sighed with relief and, with Tunji carrying my suitcase on his head and herding me through the throng ahead of us, I was finally out of the airport and in David's arms.

David introduced me to Peter who said, "Madame. You are welcome. How you dey? I am coming." With that he bowed slightly then ran off at a trot to get the car.

David scrunched up his eyes: "Is that actually you—or an apparition?"

"Kiss me, you fool."

We held that first kiss for a very long time, though it was not nearly long enough.

"I do believe it is really you," he said.

I handed him the duty-free liter bottle of Johnnie Walker Black, his favorite Scotch. He smiled. "I knew there was a reason I wanted you to come."

Peter brought the Volvo around. David put my suitcase in the boot and opened the back door. "Tonight, Peter, I will sit here next to the lady."

Peter grinned. "Yes, Masta." Had Peter just called David "Master"—and earlier had he called me "Madame"? Had I just learned my first lesson about the lingering effects of colonialism in West Africa? Did I have special status simply by having white skin?

Between Murtala Muhammed International Airport and the house on Ikorodu Road were miles of chaos and clutter. Vibrantly-dressed people darted here and there, moving singly and in waves. Cement buildings jammed against each other. Tables of goods lined the road and alcoves in front of the ubiquitous squat buildings. We passed a jumble of hand-painted signs. Cars and bicycles and trucks and buses moved slowly and stopped and honked and moved again, then, once again, stopped. Rusty tin roofs peered over great mountains of trash and rubble. Yet I took in very little during the hour it took to travel those few miles. I leaned against David and relaxed into his arms, euphoric because this moment had finally arrived. His face leaned into mine, and the second and third kisses were much longer than the first.

Peter jumped out and opened the gate into the driveway. The barefoot "watchnight" hopped off a bench and lit a flashlight. He wore an open, loose white cotton shirt, a buba, descending past his knees, and an embroidered blue fila, the traditional cap. He grinned and stood aside as Umaru, the steward, welcomed us at the door with a warm smile. Umaru was a handsome man wearing a short-sleeved white shirt over khaki pants. His face was broad with a neatly-trimmed mustache, animated eyes. He took my bag from Peter and welcomed me in a quiet, assured voice. "Madame," he said. "I am happy you have come to Nigeria."

Then he turned to David. "Of course there is no power, Master. But dinner will be ready when you want to eat."

There it was again: "Master, Madame." How much separateness did this portend?

David looked at me. "Are you hungry?" I shook my head. "In an hour, Umaru."

Downstairs in this simple but serviceable house was a living room, dining room, kitchen and offices. David took my bag from Umaru and ushered me up to the second floor sitting room. He lit some of the many candles on a plain wooden coffee table flanked by two overstuffed chairs, each upholstered in a cluttered pattern of turquoise, white and maroon rosettes. The sitting room opened up onto a balcony protected from the street by closely set iron bars. From the sitting room, doors led to the bathroom and bedrooms, painted blue-gray and furnished with double beds, plain bedside tables and matching dressers. Café-length curtains in a pattern of British-style cornucopias spilling forth apples and pears and grapes and lemons were drawn against the barred windows but did not mask the rising and falling sound of cars and horns and voices.

David showed me an empty closet and drawer, but we had better things to do than unpack.

I was there, with David, finally there. And I realized from the start that every moment of every hour together would be tinged, for me, at least, by the wonder of actually being together after three emotionally tumultuous months.

◆

Though nothing moved quickly in Lagos, the next few days went by in a brisk cacophony of sights, sounds and the ever-present smell of open sewers. Each day David showed me a different part of Lagos. He said he wanted me to know all aspects of the city in order to make my decision about returning.

We shopped downtown at the Indian-run Kingsway, at Leventis, the Greek-owned supermarket, and the Swiss-owned UTC where we indulged in croissants and New Zealand lamb and French cheeses. We went to the docks to buy shrimp off the boats and to the Federal Palace Hotel on Victoria Island for lunch among chiefs and their wives, each couple dressed in richly-embroidered agbadas and headdresses, often in matching fabrics. Afterwards we browsed the carvings displayed by craftsmen on the front lawn and bargained arduously for a ceremonial sword in a leather sheath which caught David's fancy.

Another day we shared a huge bottle of warm STAR beer at the poolside bar of the EKO Holiday Inn off the Karamo Waters and Bar Beach. Beyond the hotel, in corrugated tin and cement block buildings, lived the 10,000 people of Maroko where there was no road, electricity or water.

We took the Falamo Bridge back to Ikoyi Island with its many traditional estates where tropical palms, frangipani and canna lilies bloomed and gecko lizards darted across tall iron fences topped with long glass shards.

On the Ikoyi Club tennis courts two black men in white polo shirts and shorts volleyed behind the sign on the fence that read "whites only". The golf course had oiled, black sand greens, and two of the holes ran beside the Dodon Barracks, headquarters of the military regime. Another hole skirted a residential neighborhood where an out-of-bounds shot could conceivably dislodge clothes hanging out to dry—or disturb a three-legged horse awkwardly grazing in the yard.

We toured the squash courts and read the list of Friday night movies to be held on the lawn. On the patio, a few black men and tables of white men and women were drinking Chapmans on the patio. A Chapman was made of Grenadine, bitters, blackcurrant liquor, Fanta Orange soda and Sprite, and usually garnished with an orange or lemon—or, at the Ikoyi Club, both.

One night we met an English banker and his wife for veal picatta at Antoine's, a downtown restaurant owned by a Lebanese and favored by expatriates. The tables were close together, and the restaurant was crowded even in this holiday season. There was no air conditioning, but the food was good. On the way home a sawhorse blocked the single lane coming off the bridge, and two soldiers approached us, their rifles pointed at the car. David rolled down the window and shook his head.

The taller, younger soldier leaned toward the car. "What is the purpose of your travel?" he asked. "We just want to go home," David said.

"Where are you living?"

"Ikeja. Ikorodu Road." David took a red booklet—his driver's license—from his jacket pocket and handed it to the soldier who flipped through it, turning it upside down then right side up. "This is not in order," he said. David hesitated, looked at me, my eyes surely pleading, shook his head again then reached into his pocket and pulled out a twenty naira bill and handed it to the soldier. "I believe it is now in order," David said.

The soldier palmed the money and smiled. "Ah yes, everything is good. You may pass now." He signaled to the second soldier who pulled the sawhorse aside and waved us through with his rifle.

I sighed in relief. David drummed his fist on the steering wheel and bit his lower lip in frustration.

"We got through," I said. "What would have happened if we hadn't dashed him the twenty naira?"

"We may have gotten through anyway, since they had no valid reason to stop us. They may not have even been soldiers. In this land of Robin Hoods, the powerful steal from the rich and the poor alike."

While I admired David's brave hesitation to dash the soldiers, I was still glad to have left those pointed guns behind us.

The next day at the National Museum we savored the beautiful woven textiles and batiks and the Nok terra cotta figures. We were captivated by the display of ceremonial masks—some fierce, overlaid with skin and implanted hair or teeth. We studied the elaborately carved Yoruba doors and lost-wax process bronzes from ancient Benin—and walked quickly past the bullet-riddled Mercedes Benz in which president Murtala Mohammed was assassinated the year before.

In transit each day we endured the inevitable go-slows caused by the volume of traffic, predictable accidents and small herds of gaunt long-horn cattle crossing highways to graze the median. Whenever we stopped, street vendors swarmed the car. A boy wearing a blue sailor-suit top and no pants grinned at us from atop a cement barrier; from behind a string of barbed wires another young boy held up a calendar for sale: "Jesus Saves". Beggars who may have maimed themselves hobbled forward or reached out a stub for a handout.

We carried pockets full of cash because nobody took credit cards, and the largest banknote at the time was a twenty-naira bill. In 1977, one U.S. dollar exchanged for well under one naira, though basic goods sold in stores were considerably more costly than at home. With rampant inflation, by 2010, one dollar equaled over a hundred and sixty naira. To keep the currency portable, the Central Bank of Nigeria issued fifty-naira notes in 1991; one hundred-naira notes in 1999, five hundred-naira notes in 2001 and thousand-naira notes in 2005.

Our travels through town took us across unpaved streets muddled with piles of dirt and rubbish and broken-up concrete. Where it seemed safe, I took photographs of tin-roofed shacks and rickety market stalls in the twisted strands of unpaved back streets—and of signs painted on the backs of rickety trucks: *Struggle Continues; No Money, No Friend.*

Irony and enthusiasm were equally rampant. Outside a squat building assembled from corrugated tin and scrap wood a hand-painted sign read: *The Central Commercial Institute of Typing, Shorthand, English and Book Keeping Training Center.* Another sign on a similar building read: *Same Day Photos, Duty-Free Photographic Shop; Distributor, VitaFoam Mattresses.* Stuck in the dirt next to a few old, abandoned scooters: *All For God Vulcanizer.* And down the street, in front of a dingy cement-block building, an oil drum overflowed with rotten vegetables. Beneath it an undersized chicken pecked in the dirt. A sign wired to two swaying poles leaning against the oil drum read: *Mutanda Restaurant: Dine and Drink with us and Taste the Difference.*

And everywhere—along the roads, in the city center, congregating outside stores—all those beautiful people, a jumble of tribes, of African languages; occasionally, English, the official language, but more often Pidgin: "Comot! Why you dey give me wahala?"

Young and vibrant and struggling people with their ready tempers and quick laughter and appealing earnestness—each grappling to make it successfully through another day.

Disparity upon disparity: dusty market stands maintained by immaculately dressed Yoruba women, geles exuberantly tied around their heads; the new and the rusted Mercedes Benzes; the ever-present troops with guns slung across their shoulders; the sterile, gated, expatriate compounds for employees of large foreign corporations, and the muddy back streets, mazes through which poverty slithered.

Disparity and dearth: the lack of telephones, electricity, cars that worked; banks where you could not make a deposit because there was no power to run the cash register; offices where every desk was mounded with British-style horizontal files; the black market store where you could find a can of peas; the downtown store where you could no longer buy a chicken because fertilized eggs were banned from import.

Between assessing the man I had said I would marry and the environment where he wanted me to live, I felt slightly dazed. Each day I jumped on yet a more complex roller coaster and went for another daunting ride. And each day I survived intact, satisfied—more than that—contented, even grateful—to have been invited into David's world—so exotic, so alien to mine. I liked what I saw. I liked the open smiles of the people, and admired David's respect for his Nigerian co-workers. I liked the exuberance, the pride that gave this city so much passion.

And, as only this continent can do—even this turbulent slice of the continent, this rambunctious, overpopulated city—Africa began to tug at my soul. I began to put a shape to my life, our lives together when I returned.

As I think back, I believe we both were quieter than usual that week, David assessing whether or not I would return to Nigeria and I trying to figure out what my life would be like there. And both of us were simply content to be together again. As always, his very presence stilled my anxieties. Even in that guarded house in what surely was one of the most frenzied

199

neighborhoods of West Africa, because I was with David, I felt at peace. I felt at home. Perhaps we really could generate an exceptional future together.

◆

On occasion, through the week Umaru and I worked side-by-side in the kitchen. He had been employed mostly by British men, and his menus were limited. He taught me about British terms and measures and how to turn tough tenderloins into chewable beef with several days of marinating; I taught him about varying spices and how to cook crisp vegetables.

I liked Umaru immensely and had met his wife and children who lived crowded into two small rooms behind the house. He was the youngest of ten, a Hausa, born to an Oba in Jos, Northern Nigeria. One brother was head of a pharmaceutical firm; another, an Army officer, had been executed on Bar Beach for being on the wrong side of a coup.

Occasionally he suffered from migraine headaches which he endured with the help of a bottle of nasty-smelling brown juice which was concocted by a neighborhood witch doctor.

I proposed a deal. When "the Master" found a home for us, and I returned to Lagos as his wife, I would tutor his children—each of them, individually—if he would continue to work for us in the new house. David would make sure his living quarters were larger. I had a deal.

Peter, an Igbo, said he had learned to drive while ferrying prostitutes to the line in the Biafran war. Peter, so like the rabbit, with his close-cropped curly hair and wide eyes, was young, playful, often nervous and always energetic.

♦

Christmas was on a Sunday. David had given Peter the week off to return to his village near Calabar. Friday afternoon we drove to a nearby store in Ikeja to search for something special we could find for Sunday dinner.

As we pulled out of the driveway, we saw a man's twisted body in the middle of the road a few doors down from the house. People were jumping around it; cars swerving. Nobody stopped or even looked closely at it. I was dismayed. "Why doesn't someone move him?" I asked David.

"This isn't the first body I've seen in this road. Some remain for days. I've been told that there are taboos against touching the dead which become ancestral spirits. But, more likely, I suspect some government agency is in charge of removing bodies from the street, and they haven't been notified, or they don't have a working truck."

When we came out of the store that afternoon, we discovered that the back-seat window had been smashed. And David's briefcase—the one I had given him in New York—was gone.

His passport, including the three-month working visa and health book, were inside. We'd start working on replacing the passport and visa the next week, but he wouldn't be able to get back in the country unless he either went through all the immunizations again or had the health book recreated. I promised him I would go to Life Extension in New York and beg them to reconstruct the immunization records.

That night, as on most nights, before dinner we had cocktails and threw darts at the board in the dining room. Atypically, I was winning. In the middle of the second round, he stopped and said, "You gave me that briefcase. I don't like losing it."

"Briefcases are easy to come by," I said. "I will get you another one. In fact, I saw a really nice hand-made Kelly green leather briefcase in the gift shop at the Federal Palace Hotel. You'd like it because there were several elephants in the tooling—at least I think they were elephants. And it was only a little lopsided."

He laughed and landed three darts in the bull's eye to beat me soundly.

On Christmas morning we sat beside our sparsely-decorated palm frond and opened our gifts. I had brought him rolls of film, the paperback dictionary he requested, some blank audio tapes to record, a Brooks Brothers Oxford shirt with a button-down collar and some books, including *The Hitchhiker's Guide to the Galaxy* and, from the Museum of Modern Art, the photographic anthology, *The Family of Man.*

I also created his Nobel Peace Prize, applying individual stick-on letters to parchment paper—just like art directors, pre-computer, generated headlines. I added the appropriate filigree and a gold seal and red ribbons.

He gave me a replica of an ancient bronze of a Benin queen and a Christmas card featuring a picture of a terra cotta figure from Benin, the eyes bulging and the neck wrapped in thick wire from shoulders to lips. David's message was: "Except for the occasional stiff neck everything seems to be going fine. Season's Greetings—the Oba of Ikorodu."

And, finally, in person, he asked me if I would marry him.

"I don't think I have a choice," I said. "I can't imagine being married to anyone else. And in case you have forgotten since I told you ten minutes ago, I love you very much."

"I'll keep working toward finding offices close to town, and a house on Victoria Island, so we can have our own place where you can get into Lagos for shopping and move about freely during the day. I need you to come back soon." He held me tightly and rubbed his hand through my hair.

That afternoon we took the water taxi from the Federal Palace Hotel to Tarkwa Beach. David carried towels and suntan lotion in a British Airways flight bag atop his head, Nigerian-style, and was wearing a pair of yellow Bermuda shorts, his legs so long the hem rose far above his knees. I couldn't keep my eyes from him, this tall, adventurous man whom I then knew I would follow to Africa, and probably anywhere else he might want to go.

We walked in the sand along the shore, watching a fisherman cast his net into the surf. Giant lagoon crabs emerged from the water and, on ten raised legs, each proportionally as long as David's, scuttled across the sand.

When we had walked about half a mile, David stopped abruptly. "Turn around," he said. "Don't look back."

But, of course, I did look back at David walking toward a body, the second we'd seen that week, this man evidently washed ashore. Flies and crabs were crawling over him. David returned and put his arm around me. "It's a rough place," he said. "I worry about you being here."

I shook my head. "David, I can live here—as long as I have you."

It was a rough place, but I liked it for its energy and determination. When I returned, I would generate a life beyond work for the two of us. and I might even be able to make a positive impact on a few Nigerian lives.

In later years, he would laugh, and say he had held his breath for those ten days, not believing that I could actually like Lagos, that I would want to return. Would I have returned, would I have thrust myself into the chaos and danger, had he not been there to catch me when I grew discouraged or dismayed? Would I have returned had he not been there to laugh with me at the absurdities or share my feeling of being powerless in the face of such overwhelming hardship? I am not that brave.

♦

Umaru, a Muslim, was making us his first—and our first—Christmas dinner. I arranged a spray of soft pine branches on the table, and David lit four slim green candles, the only light in the room. The turkey was overcooked, the skin black; the yams white, as were all Nigerian yams. With no power, no air conditioning, the room was stifling. Umaru had worked hard to please us on this, our first, our most important and—despite or because of the discomfort, the less-than-perfect meal, the body lying on the beach and the one still lying in the road—our most memorable Christmas day.

Chapter Twenty-One

Within this room,
carpet unraveling
beneath my restive feet,
curtains sagging on
thin white rods
are all the lives

I ever lived—
abridged
between a Balsa mask,
winged eyebrows flying
from a flattened nose,
your Nobel prize,
my guitar,
E-string busted,

a diploma,
juju doll,
my father's rifle, a book
that needs to be rewritten
and the photograph one
of us took:
she's maybe ten,

a purple rag flung into
a dented laundry pail,
thin dress soiled
from jungle berries,
a smile wide enough
to beg poetry to dance
upon her bared tongue.

I left Lagos at 7:00 in the evening to fly back to New York on Pan Am with stops at the transit lounges of Abidjan, Ivory Coast; Robertsfield, Liberia; and Dakar, Senegal. I arrived two hours late on a very cold January morning, dropped my suitcases at home and took a cab directly to the office.

As I fumbled through the pile of papers on my desk, new methods in merchandising toilet paper or the December sales of Life Savers in Alabama seemed far less important to me than how to sell enough yams to survive in Apapa.

On the sixth of January I wrote David: "I am beginning to have a new outlook on life. I can say that I love you very much and believe I would be very happy going through life with you, but, more importantly, I can also say that what I have felt this far is an experience worth it in itself. I guess it's called acceptance. And truly caring."

Two days later, I wrote again:

"Today I was able to buy two rolls of copper wire to send to you, two bottles of tonic water, two Chinua Achebe novels, turn on electric lights, make a long-distance phone call, kill seven roaches and walk in the sleet and snow. I was also able to reconstruct the enclosed immunization book.

"On the other hand, I was unable to charter a boat to the beach, drink Orange Squash, buy a goat, perspire, dash anyone, feed any chickens, choke on TomatoPep, visit a witch doctor, watch anyone pee on the street, get lost in Apapa, go to twelve stores without seeing peanut butter, laugh with you, look at you, touch you. So what's so great about New York?

"In your next assignment beyond Lagos, you will probably accomplish more in less time than you ever did in your lifetime, just for the sheer amazement of seeing things happen. The problem is that the results will seem irrelevant because, in comparison to Lagos, everything is irrelevant.

"Just in case it's slipped your mind: I love you."

♦

By mid-January, blizzards pounded the Midwest, and tornados and high winds pummeled the east coast. New York was slapped by snow, sleet, flooding and icing. Within a week, the cycle was repeated. Residential streets remained unplowed. Parts of Long Island went without power.

Mentally I tried to escape to Lagos, but it was too damn cold to even imagine the sunburned streets of Africa.

That freezing day, the twentieth of January, we served Hirschfeld with yet another temporary restraining order over the passenger elevator. That afternoon, heat ceased flowing through our building, and, like birds startled by winter, the tenants shuffled through the lobby puffed up in winter sweaters and coats. I wore my down snowmobile jacket.

Hirschfeld claimed that the furnace fuel pump was broken. Lincoln, the philosophy professor, and Harold, the shoe executive, went to the basement to ask the superintendent about the problem. The fuel gauges were empty. I arranged for emergency fuel delivery and the furnace fired right up—until the fuel ran out again.

The next morning I received a call from Lee Lynch with the Minneapolis advertising agency, Carmichael-Lynch. He asked me to join him for a drink after work that evening. I had known Lee for many years, and admired what he and his agency had done creating the Arctic Cat snow-mobile brand. Arctic Cat owners were beyond loyal, and a lot of that was due to the aura created by Carmichael-Lynch. This dynamic, creative agency, with its spirited and eager young professionals, was also producing exciting work for impressive clients: Midwest McDonalds and Ford dealers; new products for 3-M, Beatrice Foods and General Mills. I looked forward to seeing Lee again.

Wearing a pair of cords and black sweater, Lee sat back in a red leather club chair at the hotel bar and stroked his beard, waiting for my response. He had just offered me the vice-presidency I had promised myself I'd attain before age thirty-five. A dream job. A very nice salary, bonuses, car allowance, partnership opportunity. He would pay my moving expenses.

While editing the snowmobile magazine I had spent a lot of time in Minneapolis, and I liked the city and the people I'd met. Outside of New York, maybe Atlanta, I probably knew more people who lived in Minneapolis than anywhere else. The city flanked both sides of the Mississippi River, and was surrounded by twenty lakes. It was home to the Tyrone Guthrie Theater and the University of Minnesota. To me it was the New York of the Midwest or, more accurately, perhaps, the young, vibrant New York of a previous century. The Carmichael-Lynch offices were in the elegant old Pillsbury mansion; the atmosphere was charged with creativity. Six months ago, I might have asked if I could start on Monday.

"I'm requesting a year's contract and a two-year moral commitment," Lee said.

I shook my head. His offer was more than fair, and if I made the move, I would want to commit fully. The job would be challenging, stimulating, and a whole lot of work, but, if nothing else, I had plenty of energy. Maybe I could do it.

"Lee," I said. "I am honored. You create exceptional, really exciting work, and I would be extremely proud to be part of your team, but— oh, my. Right now, I just don't know what to say."

He paused and looked at me thoughtfully.

"Sally, are you involved with someone?" I sat back, smiled and nodded. "I'll pay his moving expenses, too."

"He is building a paper mill in Nigeria."

Lee just laughed. "No problem. I'll still pay his moving expenses. Look, I know Minneapolis is a long way from New York, but you'll have trips back here."

I imagined myself living in a nice condo in Minneapolis, and maybe keeping a studio apartment in New York as well. I imagined the excitement of producing innovative work which Carmichael-Lynch and their clients would appreciate. I envisioned leisurely weekend afternoons on a nearby lake surrounded by tall pines. I pretended I was already married to David. In Minneapolis. Hell, weren't there a lot of paper mills in Minnesota?

"Come out and meet with us in our office, then make the decision," Lee said.

I wanted this job. I wanted David. Either way, I'd set sail on a channel leading into an unfamiliar, maybe calm, maybe dangerous sea. And I realized I would have to choose one passage or the other—I could not have both.

We decided I would fly to Minneapolis on Friday, the seventeenth of February, piggybacking on a planned Chicago trip. Lee left for the airport. I went home in a perplexed daze.

I also went home to a flooded closet and a building without water. Hirschfeld claimed it was due to repairing a leak. Harold, as treasurer and a member of the tenants' steering committee, had, that afternoon, deposed for yet another contempt of court affidavit against Hirshfeld, this one asking not for money, but our landlord's incarceration.

Six days later, January 27, we all received a notice from the management of 15-17 Park Avenue Operating Company accusing two members of the tenant committee of tampering with the furnace:

". . . . the sporadic problems with the heat and hot water has nothing to do with the Landlord or the staff of 15-17 Park Avenue but with a mysterious visitor or visitors in our basement during the night in areas where they do not belong."

Although the letter first stated that the visitors were mysterious, it then claimed that the superintendent asked Harold and Lincoln to leave the area on the twentieth of January, the night the heat first went off. The letter continued: "Whoever is responsible for these pranks should consider themselves advised and warned that they will be prosecuted to the fullest extent of the law if caught in areas that do not concern them. . . . Many people could be injured or killed by this foolishness."

The letter then implied that members of the Tenants Association turned off the heat to make "tenants angry due to lack of heat and hot water." I was furious. We were all furious. Two of our own had been maligned. Enough with small-bore muskets. We wanted heavy artillery: cannons, deadly iron balls.

When the tenants next met we organized a rent strike. I would notify the landlord in mid-February by letter, and we'd deposit our checks in the tenants' association account until our demands were met.

Hirschfeld retaliated by saying anyone who did not pay the rent would not have elevator access, then threatened to withhold building employee paychecks until the rent was paid.

Chapter Twenty-Two

In the fast lane
battling for a distant flag,
a lap to go or maybe ten,
a hundred, who knows
what pace to set,
who to pass or shadow
when to stop and when
to charge a little harder.

The first weekend in February, after two separate trips to Pittsburgh to meet with Arby's franchise owners, I detoured to the Pocono Mountains for the weekend on a trophy assignment for *Snow-Goer* Magazine. I recall Dee Ann Andretti spending most of the day at the stove making scrumptious fried bread, and her husband, Mario, with their children out on the frozen lake behind the cabin, engaged in an endless series of races with their powerful snowmobiles and ATVs. I joined them outside for a while, but was no match for Michael, then sixteen, or fourteen-year old Jeff, each already seriously determined to out-race the other.

In 1955, Mario's parents had emigrated from a refugee camp near Florence, Italy, to the smallish town of Nazareth, PA, and the Andretti family still lived there. But, in 1968 Mario purchased this additional playground in the Poconos for his family; he called it his "resort". There were 650 acres, a large cabin, a private lake and storage space for a sizeable collection of motorized toys.

I remember coming into the cabin and standing by the fire in the family room, an extension of the kitchen, the smell of onions and tomatoes simmering on the stove. As I sipped a brandy, the moon rose, brushing the lake with an ivory glow, and then the snow began to feather down, muting the sounds of engines still darting around the lake.

Mario, gracious, content in his home, his family and guests surrounding him, stood beside me to warm his hands by the fire. We began to talk, and while I recorded mental notes for my story, and told myself how fortunate I was to be staying in the home of one of the greatest, most respected racing drivers of all time, all I really wanted at that moment was for David to be beside me, sharing this splendid day.

♦

I would spend a more-than-splendid few days with David the very next week. He called me from Nigeria telling me he'd be in London on the eighth of February for a week-long purchasing meeting, and why didn't I come over for the weekend. We were cut off before I could reply, but when he called again from London, I already had flight reservations. On Friday I left the office at five o'clock for Kennedy airport. Since I had no more vacation time, I would have to be back in New York Monday morning. Pan Am Flight #2 would deliver me into Heathrow 6:40 Saturday morning, and Monday morning, Pan Am #1, leaving at 11:00 AM would get be back to New York a little after noon. I'd only miss half a day. Close enough.

Just as David seemed comfortable in New York and Lagos, he also seemed at home in London. We walked through peaceful, stylish St. James's Park, by Buckingham Palace, the houses of Parliament and The Royal Horse Guards. I left Harrods having purchased a smart blue sweater and scarf. We shot darts with locals at a pub in Westminster. And we talked.

Saturday night, in the hotel room, he sat beside me on the bed and reached over to stroke my hair. "You should go to Minneapolis," he said, "and meet with them. You need to make sure."

I swallowed hard, thinking this might be the beginning of another too-long separation. I lay back against the pillow, and he turned to look down at me. "A few weeks ago I received approvals for the down payments and letters of credit. This week, after the Nigerians arrive, we should have all the contracts settled. After I return, George Landegger will be in Nigeria for the board meeting which should ratify all the contracts and equipment purchases. I expect to have full signing privileges and a salary in keeping with the requirements of the chief executive of a three hundred million dollar company."

I looked up at his eyes, serious, and over at his hand—the inflexible left hand—that lay still in his lap. He had accomplished a remarkable amount in five months, and I could not have been more proud of him. I sat up again to kiss him.

"I'm not finished, woman. Stop that for a minute and listen.

"After I return from Calabar to meet with the chiefs, I should be able to again look for suitable housing in earnest." He sighed and shook his head. "But, as you well know, until I have the lease in hand, I can't be sure of anything."

"I know," I said. "It's just that. . . ."

Now he smiled that most comforting of smiles and kissed me. "I can't be sure of anything except that I love you," he said.

"So maybe I shouldn't go to Minnesota. It's not right to take their time and ask them to pay my expenses if I'm not going to seriously consider the job."

"Sally, I don't want you to choose Minneapolis over being in Lagos with me, but I want you to be absolutely sure. And you never know. I could be out of Nigeria for good before you even meet with them. So it would be nice to know there's a VP in the family to support me while I look for work."

♦

My flight was late getting into New York, and I went straight to the office. Harold called me to tell me he had received a special dispossess notice for being a nuisance. The rest of us had received regular dispossess notices. As a result, the tenants were filing yet another injunction.

The next injunction resulted in Harold being sued for "maliciously destroying" the concierge desk, even though, under court order, it was carefully dismantled. I told him I would tell Hirschfeld that David took it apart, and he could reach him in Lagos. Harold did not laugh.

We now held $18,000 in rent money in our account. When I next talked to Abe, he wanted to know whether or not I was planning to renew my lease which was up on the thirtieth of May. "That's a long way off," I said.

That Wednesday I returned from a half hour client meeting to find seven messages on my desk from tenants, newspapers, TV stations and lawyers. Instead of returning those calls, I dialed one of David's daughters. I would be in Richmond that weekend on my way to Mathews before meetings in DC, then Chicago, followed by my interview in Minneapolis. It was past time to meet the children. I wanted them to know who I was, and to know that they could trust me to love their father and respect them and their relationships with their mother. They weren't going to be available either Friday night or Monday morning.

I was disappointed that I would miss an important opportunity to learn more about their father by knowing who his children were, and even more, to assure them of my commitment to them and their father.

I began a letter to David en route from Chicago to Minneapolis. "By the time this weekend is over, I will have travelled some 26,000 air miles since mid-December and I'm beginning to feel as if I live in a 3x3 cubicle. Actually, there is an advantage as these cubicles appear to be free of roaches—and telephones."

As I entered the old stone, ivy-draped Pillsbury mansion the next morning, I was enthralled by the marble fireplaces, stained glass windows, skylights, the conference rooms furnished with antique library tables. I discovered during the interview that I was better prepared for the job than I initially imagined; my combination of magazine and advertising experience would be an advantage. I liked what I saw and who I met. I would wait for the contract to arrive.

The next Friday, February 24, we gathered again in the NY Supreme Court, and Hirschfeld was fined $6,400 for being in contempt over the 15 Park Avenue elevator. Four thousand of that would cover our past-due lawyer fee. I was elated; our efforts were finally paying off.

That Sunday I wrote David from my office. "The exterminator really did show up for a change, but it was the day I was trying to get home from London. Every roach in the building found out I was away and moved in. So this morning I lit half a dozen fumigation bombs, ran out the door, leaving a map on the floor showing the fastest roach path to Hirschfeld's office. Can't wait to get home to the stench, not to mention the job of cleaning out all the dead bodies. Can't wait to move."

In early March I received a raise—and an admonition to be a better team player within the department. I knew I was flying solo a good deal of the time, but much of my time was spent either traveling to client meetings, in client meetings or developing promotions for my own assigned accounts. Rightly or wrongly, I also felt I had understood my client's needs, and worked hard to come up with innovative solutions. With the raise, Minneapolis looked a little less attractive money-wise, but, with the reprimand, more attractive creatively.

Arby's franchise owners had just hired a new vice-president of marketing who demanded a change in the creative group one month prior to the deadline for three new commercials and a new product introduction in San Diego. However, he applauded the collateral I presented for three current promotions.

Although Coca-Cola owned the rights to the Norman Rockwell *Saturday Evening Post* covers, we managed to obtain those rights for an upcoming summer glass promotion for Arby's. We also found a new glass-printing process in Chicago which would ensure fidelity of the four-color artwork. The new Arby's VP was ecstatic.

And all of a sudden there was the strong likelihood that I would receive a promotion out of my department into the agency's Arby's group, and would be guaranteed a salary at least as attractive as the Minneapolis offer—and perhaps the chance for a vice-presidency as well.

Minneapolis was making less sense. Yet if I were offered and accepted this new position, I would feel obligated to put in at least six months.

Optionally, I could turn it down and stay clearly locked in the holding pattern I'd been flying for the past six months.

What excuse could I offer for refusing a promotion? And, if everything fell apart with David, would I have opportunities as attractive as these two? My rational pendulum swung toward New York and accepting the promotion.

My best friend, my confidante at the agency at the time, was Helen, the telex operator who, if necessary, would try all day, using all available means, to help me send a message to Nigeria. When David sent me a letter suggesting that we get married in April, Helen transmitted my response back: "Minneapolis resistible. Abe would love it. I'd love it. I love you. When and where?"

My emotional pendulum had shifted back toward Africa.

Throughout the rest of March, I was still flying weekly to Pittsburgh and/or Chicago, and involved in arduous late-into-the-night meetings to come up with a workable compromise for the building. During our next court appearance, an alleged tenant testified that she agreed with the proposed changes on behalf of the "Committee for a Better Building". We sent her two registered letters using the address she claimed in the 15 Park Avenue building, and both were returned as "addressee unknown."

A core group of tenants became so angry they would accept no compromise. I resigned as president of the association. My resignation was ignored.

The fight went on.

THE CITY OF NEW YORK
OFFICE OF THE MAYOR
NEW YORK, N.Y. 10007

March 9, 1978

Honorable Edward J. Greenfield
Judge
Supreme Court of the State of New York
60 Centre Street
New York, New York

Dear Judge Greenfield:

I was dismayed to learn that my name appeared in a letter, dated January 20, 1978, sent to you by Elie Hirschfeld, who represents the landlord at 15 Park Avenue.

His communication states that a letter of support for the landlord's demands came from "Mr. Harold Koch, the brother of the mayor of New York City." I know that this tactic will not affect your judgement, but I would like you to know that the landlord's use of my name is offensive to me. It can only have been used to create an unjustified impact on the course of events. I should add that my brother is an independent person who makes his own decisions, just as I do.

Sincerely,

Edward I. Koch
MAYOR

Chapter Twenty-Three

No man could hold
that dazzling woman
bolting from love's gentle slope
to climb a higher cliff, splashing
head-first into
an unfamiliar pool,
claiming it for her sisters.

And, yes, I followed her
without a word
of thanks
until a hand, stronger
than my own, reached into
the murky water, and a voice,
surer than my own, whispered:
Come. Together you and I
are so much more
than you or I alone.

When I returned home from work on Thursday afternoon, March 23rd, a telegram was waiting for me: "URGENT ARRIVING JFK FRIDAY ON PAA 191 LOVE DAVID."

He would leave Lagos at eight o'clock at night, stopping in Dakar and Monrovia, and get into New York at 6:35 Friday morning—Good Friday.

I cleaned up my apartment as best as I could, set the alarm for 5:30 the next morning and was outside the customs area as planeloads of weary passengers trickled through. Finally a group of Africans appeared, dressed in colorful agbadas and caftans, and right behind them, the man I was waiting for, his head ducked down, looking at me sideways with a "Who is that woman?" smile.

He dropped his suitcase and hugged me. I stood on my toes for a kiss. "Right here in Kennedy Airport?" he asked.

I laughed. "Yes, right here." He kissed me, and when we could hold it no longer, I asked: "Will you marry me?"

"Right here in Kennedy Airport?"

"If necessary," I said.

"Yes, you crazy woman. But there are infinitely better places for a wedding."

In the cab, he teased me, saying he had only come to New York because Jimmy Carter was arriving in Lagos the next weekend, and he was worried about reprisals against Americans during the president's visit. I told the cab driver to drop me off at my office, gave David my apartment keys and sent him home to get some sleep.

"If you meet me at the Oyster Bar at 12:30 we can have lunch, and, by then, I will have figured out how to escape the office for the rest of the day."

We spent that rainy Easter Sunday making plans to be married in London in late May and called our families to tell them. David's father's voice resonated as joy. The delight in his mother's response was celebration in itself. She said she'd make flight and hotel reservations as soon as we had a firm date. My mother was pleased that I would be in England during at least part of her planned trip. I promised Dad I would be in Mathews two weekends from then and, yes, he could throw me a going-away party. David's daughter Shelley assured me that she would be available when I went through Richmond that weekend.

Next we called my good friend Bonnie and I told her I would need a matron of honor. Yes, she and her husband, Ellis, would come to London.

Thus ended seven months of theatrics, of ecstasy and agony: seven months of wondering whether or not I was in love with an actor who'd appeared briefly on the stage only to disappear before the next show; seven months of bracing for a heartbreaking finale. There would be no more tryouts to determine which role I wanted to play: the career woman, feminist with an admittedly muted bullhorn, or the accommodating bride, her success in life no longer measured by what she, alone, might achieve.

Now, on this most blessed of Easter Sundays, the curtain had dropped on an act which promised ever-after happiness.

And we would be happy. I had just made the most serious commitment of my life—an allegiance that would last forever—and nothing—*nothing*—would keep me from honoring it.

Over the next month and a half all I needed to do was figure out how and if we could legally be married in England; go to work, then give notice; sell some furniture; put some in storage; pack; vacate my apartment; do my tax returns; find a place to stay in London; find a place to get married; confirm the date with everyone who would attend; arrange a place for a reception; buy a wedding dress; have a physical; revise my will and power of attorney; say goodbye to my father and to a few dozen friends in New York; get to know my future stepchildren; obtain an airline ticket and a new three-month Nigerian visa. But first I had to extricate myself from the million-dollar lawsuit which my landlord, Abe Hirschfeld, had just filed against me as president of the tenant's association, now holding $30,000 in rent-strike money.

All David had to do was run his company, find us a place to live in Lagos—and show up at the wedding.

Chapter Twenty-Four

At the summit
who looks back
at the fractured road,
the arroyos leapt
just a few paces ago
when further on
another crest—and then
unquestionably another.
Unquestionably
another.

The wedding would be in England for many reasons. London was between New York and Lagos. A London wedding would please my Anglophile mother and honor my British grandmother. My father would not travel overseas, which erased the probable conflicts with my mother. We could have an intimate ceremony, shared with a few good friends, David's parents and my mother. The children would be at the center of a later celebration.

In order to be married in London, one of us was required to register as a resident in the district where the ceremony would occur at least fifteen days prior to the wedding. Initially we thought David's previous trips might suffice, but the British consulate told me that one of us needed a continuous stay before the ceremony. I would have to arrive no later than the eleventh of May if we were to be married on Saturday, the twenty-seventh.

The company leased a flat in Sloane Court in the Royal Borough of Kensington and Chelsea where David suggested I claim residency. Even if the flat were otherwise occupied during part of my stay, I could still use it as a valid address and stay in a Chelsea hotel if necessary.

I wanted a church wedding and imagined being married in a chapel of a grand cathedral with the certificate signed by a bishop of the Church of England. Of course I knew, since David's previous marriage had been dissolved in divorce, the Church of England would never consent to our marriage in any of its sanctuaries, whether imposing or humble. I began searching for other churches, starting with the London phonebook. Perhaps the Unitarians would be more understanding, but, evidently, there were no Unitarians in Chelsea—at least no Unitarian church. But there was a Methodist church. I called the church then wrote to the minister, Rev. Horton, pleading my case, and asked an Episcopal priest I knew to contact him on our behalf.

Reverend Horton responded: "The Methodist church believes that marriage is for life and also understands that for some people, mistakes are made in their marriage. The divorced person has to demonstrate to the local minister that his or her previous marriage was a genuine mistake and that he or she has serious intentions for the anticipated marriage. Furthermore anyone being married in the Chelsea Methodist Church is required to pay the fee of £34 and undertake to meet with me for at least four occasions to discuss their relationship and their marriage."

He then equivocated and said that, provided he could meet with both of us once prior to the wedding and saw no glaring reasons why we should not be married, he would conduct the ceremony at two o'clock on May twenty-sixth.

How could David tell the minister that a marriage that resulted in the birth of five children was a mistake, at least at the onset? And what would we do if we and our families and friends arrived in London for a wedding which could not be held should the minister find us unacceptable?

A few days later I received a second letter from Rev. Horton saying that he had mixed up the dates and he would be on holiday that week. I saw no choice but to opt for a civil ceremony.

In my mind there were two types of civil ceremonies: Vegas glitz and New York let's-just-get-it-over-with. Once, in Vegas, I interviewed Michael Parks who starred in the television series *Then Came Bronson*. That episode included a scene at a wedding chapel. After a dozen takes, I felt I had been to a dozen Las Vegas weddings. Vegas was the right choice for a number of my friends, and for innumerable movie stars, some of whom were married in the chapel of their choice on a regular basis, but garish red hearts and cheap brass filigree did not create the atmosphere I chose to consecrate a serious commitment.

I wanted at least a touch of pomp and an overtone of solemnity—enough, at least, to dignify the most important promise I would ever make, a promise meant to be kept until and probably long after a death parted us. I should not have worried. A civil service in London is extraordinarily civil.

◆

A little less than a month before I had to leave, I flew into Richmond and finally met two-fifths of my future step-children. Daughters two and three—Shelley (Bub) and Patricia (Tod)— captivated me: Bub, vivacious, dark eyes large and expressive, and Tod, red-haired, perspicacious, a ready laugh, both charming and charmingly skeptical. They were beautiful and bright young college women. I was impressed. I wanted to love them, champion them, spoil them, be as good a friend as I could be to them.

Here were David's children, his family, and, possibly by association, they would become somewhat mine as well. I sat across from them in a booth at a predictable restaurant and listened as they expressed their unpredictable goals: oceanography or maybe marine biology for Tod; radio/television for Bub. I believed I could find some connections for Bub in New York, and urged her to let me help.

"You remind me of our mother," Bub said. I could make no response, wondering how we might be alike. I knew their mother was an extraordinarily beautiful woman; more glamorous than me. I was told she'd been a homecoming queen. I knew she was smart, and had birthed five children, each following the last as soon as possible. She had cared for them while their father pursued a career to support his growing family.

Her life had been radically different from mine, enveloped by infants and toddlers at a time when I was just trying to figure out what life held for me in New York. I'd been told that, when the children were moving toward independence, she sought independence as well.

We ordered dessert, and I asked the girls the question most important to me. "So—do I have your approval for marrying you father?"

"It's better to live with someone," Tod said. Bub concurred.

I laughed. "No, I'm in this for the long term."

Bub's eyes grew wide, her mouth teasing. "So, can we come to the wedding?"

"The wedding is too complicated. I don't even know where it is going to be, or exactly when. I only know that it will be somewhere in London around the end of May. But you can come see us at Christmas break—all of you. How does Spain or Paris sound?"

"Cool!" Bub said. "Pastries and all that wine!"

"It will happen," I said.

When I left the girls, I felt comfortable about them; more, I felt elated. They were bright, open, interesting, very much like their father.

That weekend I said good-bye to my own father. He told me he would soon be returning to Terre Haute, Indiana to marry his third bride, Zelma, his high-school sweetheart. He would be leaving the only house where I knew him as an adult. But, this time, I would be leaving him first, and my own forthcoming marriage might even have been one of the many factors in his own decision.

He threw a cocktail party and invited some thirty retired friends who were inquisitive, well-wishing and kind. Before leaving Mathews, he gave me a wedding gift—a small diamond pendant on a white-gold chain. I promised him I would wear it on my wedding day.

As I pulled out of the driveway with Dad waving good-bye, I stopped for a moment, capturing his image as a camera might; I took a deep breath and waved back, wondering if I would ever see him again.

When I returned to New York, Josh called me with good news: the million dollar lawsuit Hirschfeld had filed against me had been dismissed. I was relieved, though I wondered what Hirschfeld thought he could realize from my assets: half a closet of undeveloped film plus a round of plywood sitting on an old truck tire, a barber chair, a few shelves of books, illustrations by relatively-unknown artists, a brass headboard, an unplayed banjo and a typewriter with the "8" and "A" keys missing.

I gave my notice at work and told Hirschfeld I would not renew my lease, due to expire the end of May. Lou would take over my apartment.

My British Airways flight would leave the evening of the eighth, a Monday. The first two nights I would stay at the Cadogan Hotel, Sloane Street, Knightsbridge then find some other alternative.

On the second of May, Jim Hayes, the managing director of Parsons and Whittemore, Lyddon, telexed me that the Sloane Square flat would be available through most of May, though his daughter would be there on the fourteenth through the twenty-third. I wasn't sure when David would arrive.

A week before I was scheduled to leave I had a complete physical and a gynecology exam. The gynecologist called late Friday, May 5, to tell me that my pap smear showed an abnormality. She told me I might have mild dysplasia.

"How urgent is this?" I said. "Don't you remember? I'm leaving in three days to be married in London. Then I'm going to Nigeria."

"Find a gynecologist in London. Don't wait six months. Okay? If it's more than what I suspect, they may want to do a biopsy, but I'm sure it will be fine. Is there someplace I can mail the report?

I gave her the address of David's office and assured her that I would find a practitioner in London.

Mild. She said it was mild. I would treat it as mild until I knew otherwise. I was getting married. Nothing mild could interfere with the anything-but-mild life I was about to assume.

The night before I left, some friends took me to dinner at The Brasserie. Toni, who worked at the Motion Picture Association, had obtained director Robert Altman's signature on a pre-release packet for "A Wedding," a comedy due out in August. It was the perfect gift.

I returned that night to an apartment empty except for a mattress and phone. My cameras, makeup and clothes were sitting atop the suitcase I would pack in the morning. As I walked across the living room, my too-loud footsteps reverberated behind me. Then the phone rang in the bedroom; it sounded invasive, eerie, like a phone ringing in a room where nobody lives. I answered it, and my mother said:

"So, are you all set to go?"

"Yes. It's a little bare in here. And I'm a little nervous."

"Are you worried about David?"

"Mom, come on. If it were anyone but David I would be a whole lot more nervous. There's nothing left in the apartment, that's all. It's like someone else is about to walk out the door and leave me behind."

"Well, I just thought you might be nervous about David. When will he get to London?"

"We'll both be at the airport to pick you up, Mother. I'll see you in a week."

Three minutes after she hung up, Elliott Galloway called: "I just spoke to your mother and called because I was concerned."

Only later did I realize why Mother might have been so anxious. It was May 7, her anniversary. She didn't mention it that night, but she must have been thinking of my father, and the unhappy ending to their marriage.

I had received only one phone call, two cables and one new letter from David after he returned to Lagos following our Easter weekend. Maybe I should have been worried, but he had been so constant and persuasive in his affections, so unwavering in his intentions, that I fully believed he would arrive in London long before the expected wedding.

I was worried, instead, about who I was destined to become. I was leaving a future I might be able to predict with some certainty for one I could only scantly imagine.

That night, as I lay on the bare mattress, I thought back through my nearly thirteen years in New York City. Before I arrived I had met few people whose backgrounds differed substantially from mine, but, during my first year, having discovered so many people from such a wide variety of cultures, I felt I had encountered more of the world than in all my previous twenty years. I relished those encounters.

I thought about the crazy jobs I'd had; the nights at the office when others had left, and I stayed on. I had worked so hard, and accepted so many assignments solely to prove myself worthy of advancement. I thought of the places I'd been able to travel simply because I was willing to go. From Quebec City to the Yukon, Los Angeles to Vero Beach. I thought of the men and women I'd befriended, and the several men I tried to love.

As a woman, it was difficult to command a job equivalent to the title and salary offered a man with comparable or less experience, the excuse always being that a woman would leave to get married. I had finally proved them right. But didn't men leave their jobs, if not for marriage, at least for other jobs?

I recalled the evening when, around six o'clock, Cook Neilson and I were tossing a Frisbee in the hallway outside the *Cycle* Magazine office, and the president, Bill Ziff, walked by. I thought we would be reprimanded, but he smiled at us, fondly. We must have seemed to him like youngsters who needed a bit of recess before getting back to work.

And we *were* youngsters. We were hopeful young. Determined young. Confident young. Not much frightened us, and we felt we could achieve anything we desired.

My last night in New York I knew that, though my goals had changed, my determination was as strong as it had ever been. Now I would have a nation in West Africa to comprehend; optimistically, a few people there to urge toward their potential; stepchildren to nurture; hopefully a child of my own. I could still dream of being published in *The New Yorker*; of writing good books. Most importantly, because we were about to make the most serious of commitments to each other, I would do all I could to love a man more than I had ever loved anyone before.

♦

Two of my friends, Mary Louise and Jill, said they wanted to take me to the airport. They rang the bell to my apartment; I picked up my suitcase and donned the Burberry raincoat Mary Louise insisted I buy. ("No matter where in the world you go, no matter what season, if you are wearing a Burberry, the doorman at the hotel will understand," she said.) It was the most expensive garment I had ever purchased, a small fortune per each of the many buttons and each epaulet, but at least I would be understood by the doormen of the world, though I can't imagine now why that was important then.

I descended to the lobby with them, and waiting outside was a long, black limousine. And within the limousine was a bottle of champagne. What a send-off!

◆

The night before the wedding we gathered for dinner in the bell tower of the Belfry Club—a church converted into a private dining club— David's idea. Even if we could not have an ecclesiastical wedding, we would at least enjoy the ambiance of an old church. Phoebe gave me a pearl ring that had belonged to her mother and a nosegay of flowers to carry at the wedding. Something old, something new. My mother gave me a bracelet with small turquoise stones that had belonged to her mother. Something blue.

My dear friend, Bonnie, stayed with me that night at the Chelsea flat so I could air any lingering worries, reiterate my intentions to fully love and respect David, emphatically claim that our marriage would be forever successful. We talked late into the night, girl talk, and she loaned me a garter. Something borrowed.

The next morning we took a cab to the Chelsea Registry. I wore a cream muslin two-piece dress I had bought at B. Altman's in New York. The top draped my shoulders with a lace-fringed shawl collar; the calf-length skirt was softly pleated; thin cream and lavender ribbons tied at the waist. We would arrive unseen by the groom until the ten o'clock wedding.

The Registrar, in his formal morning dress, greeted us at the door and ushered our guests into the golden Brydon Room with its tall draped windows, crystal chandeliers and upholstered mahogany chairs.

Bonnie and I were directed to the bride's antechamber for the pre-ceremony formalities. It wasn't until I entered the Brydon Room that I saw David, standing beside the registrar's desk in the double-breasted pin-striped suit he'd bought at Harrods a week before. And then he was holding my hands and declaring that there was no lawful impediment to our being joined in matrimony. I looked into his eyes, focused solely on mine as he repeated after the registrar: "I, David, take thee, Sally, to be my lawfully wedded wife." And as sure as I had ever been of any words in my life, I said, "I, Sally, take thee, David, to be my lawfully wedded husband."

I slipped the gold band I had bought two days earlier at Mappin & Webb onto the ring finger of his right hand; he eased a matching band against the small four-diamond engagement ring on my left hand, and we both repeated, after the

Registrar: "I give you this ring as a symbol of our marriage and a token of my love."

I cry at weddings. I cry at the very mention of weddings because I see in each couple standing side by side an abundance—though so fragile an abundance—of potentiality. I am crying now. At the wedding held at ten o'clock in the morning on May 27, 1978 at the Royal Borough of Kensington and Chelsea Registry, London, I did not shed a single tear.

We were man and wife, woman and husband, two separate people joined together by love, by law, and I would always believe, even without the benefit of the church, we were joined by God.

We left the building to a cascade of rice which Bonnie tossed into our pathway. At the Penthouse suite of the Dorchester Hotel on Park Lane we greeted our guests again—my mother, David's parents; Bonnie and Ellis from New York; Jim and Libby Hayes and Hugh and Francoise Calder from London, plus the collection of British cousins my mother had enticed us to include.

The gilded and mirrored reception room spilled out into a patio decorated with ornate statues overlooking Hyde Park. We were served cocktails and an assortment of cold and hot hors d'ouvres. Fortnum and Mason delivered the small, traditional fruitcake with marzipan and stiff, smoothly-carved royal icing.

After the reception, I went back to the Royal Westminster where David was staying, and leisurely, luxuriously, we consummated our marriage. A few hours later, we met his mother and father for dinner in the restaurant of the hotel. While the name of the hotel has changed, the restaurant has not. When I last visited London there was still a table by the window where we all sat together that night.

The next morning, David and I left for Nigeria.

As the plane passed over the Balearic Islands, headed toward Algiers, the co-captain came down the aisle. He stopped to speak to me. "I understand," he said, "that you would like to join us for a little while up front."

I turned to David, puzzled, and he shrugged. "I just thought you might want to see what it was like flying a 747."

I spent thirty minutes in the cockpit of an airliner flying over Algerian desert, watching the dials, asking questions, observing a continent pass below me—all because of the thoughtfulness of a man who had become my husband a little over twenty-four hours before.

David in New York, 1977

David with a colleague, Nigeria, 1978

Umaru and his family;
Ikorodu Road, 1977.

London, 1978: Phoebe on the Dorchester terrace;
Tony and Sally outside the Grenadier Pub.

Mother at the wedding. Dad.

The bride and groom.

Early construction at the site; a nearby home.

*A young girl returning with laundry
from the stream near Oku Iboku, 1979;
a yam gatherer from the North.*

Chapter Twenty-Five

That May morning
your mother squeezed
my hand with a promise:
we'd grow closer
with each year. We didn't know
she wouldn't survive
a season. Yet later—

when we navigated
Lekki Lagoon, anchored
one starless night
in Muir, followed a lioness
across a kopje, chased sunset over
the Matterhorn—
I thanked her for the gift
of you—and yes,
each time
her broad hand
reached out
to cover mine.

We spent two more years in Nigeria. Though our
marriage had been delayed until David could
procure suitable housing, for the first six months
we lived in various rooms of the Eko Holiday Inn,
directly across the street from our unfinished
home. Several times we were forced to stay with

friends as the entire hotel would be occupied by the military government. Each time we returned to the hotel we installed our dart board behind a painting and set up a dark room in the bathroom.

We found good friends among Nigerians and expatriates from the US, the UK and France, and I tutored Umaru's children until they soared to the head of their classes. It didn't take much to give them an advantage; I was delighted with their progress.

We acquired a German Shepherd puppy which we named The Dis'ting and a small British stern-drive boat we named *Vroom*. On most Sunday afternoons we met our friends at the beach to play Scrabble and bocce and to swim. With Dis'ting, we made a day-long boat trip through the mandrake groves of the Lagos Lagoon to the Lekki Lagoon and on to Iwopin for an overnight visit to the paper mill there.

Once the two of us drove north, all the way to Kano, passing red mud huts, small villages and field after field of yams, old women gathering them and carrying them home on their heads. At a motel in Kaduna, we asked what was available at the restaurant. "Rice," said the young man behind the counter.

"Rice and what else?" David asked.

"Rice."

We pulled out our kerosene stove and, under a single slight bulb, put together a freeze-dried meal in our squalid, yellow-green room.

On our visits to the site I made friends with the Nigerian children who accompanied me on long walks through the bush and taught me about their world of coconut palms and native medicines and ancestral shrines.

In Lagos I busied myself with photography and writing; supported local artists through an expatriate soiree which featured their work once a month. I corralled a roomful of children to create scores of candles for the women's club to support their local charities.

And I scrounged for food. On an average of three times a week we housed overseas corporate visitors, including David Alexander Cospatrick Douglas-Home, son of the former prime minister and now the fifteenth Earl of Home. He was the only one of our guests to chase butterflies across our lawn. He was also the only one of our guests to arrive at dinner in a suit and tie.

Two of the children met us in Paris at Christmas, and three came to Lagos during their summer break from school.

Our house was robbed on a regular basis. If we went into town at night, we knew we would face a road block coming home. During the dry season we flagged down a government truck and paid the driver to fill our roof tank. There was no other way to obtain water.

Why had I so unhesitatingly, so willingly, almost seamlessly assumed the position of corporate wife? Was it because I was not legally allowed to hold a job in Nigeria? Was it the best I could do in this challenging environment? Was it a way to prove myself a worthwhile partner? I believe it was simply because, together, we coped, we laughed, we loved each other and embraced the life we were living.

Some six years after we left Lagos, rolls of newsprint did emerge from the mill in Oku Iboku. For a while, at least. In 2008 the then-defunct mill was purchased by a Finish firm and, four years later, was finally schedule for startup again.

Abe Hirschfeld sold the building on Park Avenue; the lobbies were converted with a single doorman serving both sides of the building. Lou moved from my apartment to a larger one at 15 Park Avenue and was still living there the last time I visited New York.

We returned once more to Africa, our home in the small village of Mgololo, Tanzania. The house overlooked an escarpment where, at night, the only lights, except for stars, shone from the occasional cooking fire across the valley.

Prior to that, we lived in a small town on Lake Michigan, the sunsets inspiring, the atmosphere mostly mundane, then on the Connecticut River in Cornish, New Hampshire, our neighbors as invigorating as the weather.

Later we lived in Lions Bay, British Columbia, high above Howe Sound, then on a backwater bay off Puget Sound on the Olympic Peninsula in Washington State. We spent an enchanted summer traveling to Skagway, Alaska on our 28-foot Camano trawler, *Haiku*. Finally we settled nearer the children in Williamsburg, Virginia, the house a little too far for my liking from the James River or Chesapeake Bay or, even farther from the Hudson River, the Thames or the Bight of Benin.

But the children—and eleven of their children—were finally close enough to embrace.

The irregular cells discovered in the pap smear before our wedding evolved from mild to a more critical stage. I would not become pregnant. Through the years, sometimes for long periods, and sometimes only at moments which made me yearn for a child of our own, I mourned the loss of our envisioned child. With the rest of the family, we grieved the loss of David Jr. when he was not yet thirty. He died in an automobile crash.

◆

After so many seasons, so many lives lay fallen behind us, yet another season was emerging. The trees were turning rusty brown and dull yellow, stubbornly refusing to burst into color, their roots still busy soaking up warm rain which fell all summer and through September.

Still, since it was autumn, and a sunny Sunday afternoon, David and I took a sentimental journey from our home in Williamsburg to nearby Mathews County. We might have found a cluster of exuberant maples or oaks on the way, but, more than that, I was hoping to reaffirm a small slice of our past.

We crossed the York River via the Coleman Bridge and headed toward Sarah's Creek. In the Yacht Haven Marina boatyard, *Haiku,* our home that breathtaking summer we sailed to Alaska, slouched into her supporting jack stands.

That day *Haiku* looked weary, unkempt, like a horse that had been too long in pasture. We patted her on the transom and assured her that she was still loved. For a fleeting moment I wanted to buy her back. She could be my summer home tied to a dock far up a tidewater creek where I would write beautiful sentences in cadence with the ebb and flow of gentle tides.

We stopped at River's Inn for a fine lunch—crab cakes and oysters—then headed further North, up the George Washington Highway, past shopping malls, tattoo parlors and hopeful diners.

Finally we turned east toward John Clayton Memorial Highway, named not for the secretary of state under Millard Fillmore, but for a botanist who was clerk of Gloucester County for over fifty years.

Though newer homes and small businesses had sprung up along the highway, Gloucester County still exuded the texture of rural America. We travelled some ten miles, past Eppa Soles Road and Chapel Neck. Just ahead on the right was the pristine building locals used to call—maybe still do—the white Black church. There we turned onto North River Road.

The "Oakland Farm" sign was gone, and in its place were two hand-lettered street numbers. There were no warnings against trespassing, so we turned into the long driveway. On the left, we passed the raw, upended roots from a large fallen tree, then broken fences, a speckled lop-eared goat, an abandoned car. On the right, a large RV rested in a large plowed field, and near the fork in the driveway was a small stable with the forgettable names of absent horses painted above each empty stall.

Through the trees we glimpsed the North River, and beside it the large, gracious pre-Civil War house protected by its broad front porch and white Doric columns—the house where Tony and I once played eight-ball and Phoebe first introduced me to the idea of David, her son.

On the left, beyond where the driveway split, a small white home, the former caretaker's cottage, cowered among sprawling outbuildings. The contrast between the two adjoining properties was astonishing, and I wondered when and how the property was divided.

David turned around slowly, reluctantly, and, one last time, I glanced into the rear-view mirror, believing that I would see a member of the family which now resides in the big house, someone I would like immediately, simply because they lived where the Stiles once lived.

We returned to the John Clayton Highway and passed Honey Pod Lane and Fickle Fen Road, heading toward the town of Mathews. For several years I had looked without success for my father's house. Finally, by comparing his old pictures to the footprints of houses and configurations of land on Google Earth, I believed I had located his home on Put-In Creek.

I remembered the road being wider, with more homes on either side, but my memory had deceived me, for there it was, at the end of a lane, my father's home. Though now painted gray instead of barn red, I recognized the workshop and the porch, the little dock, and—yes!—the roses—or sons and daughters of those original roses—so many roses which Dad planted and cultivated some forty years ago.

We got out of the car and walked down the road for a better view of the house and water. Though it was October, the maple leaves were stubbornly green, and the roses still blooming—there, in that long patch, and in that circular bed, beneath a bird feeder, and there, climbing a trellis by the door.

Dad bought this house then rebuilt and expanded it himself. I recalled the old kitchen and a second one next to it in the new addition. He valued this house, and it was apparent that someone valued it still, had improved it, tended to it and tended to all those roses, once Dad's roses, now theirs. My past existed—even bloomed.

But I also remembered how Dad had left Esther behind, alone in a nearby cemetery, her ashes beneath a single flat stone in a family plot which nobody else would ever occupy.

If I lost David, would I search out an earlier love as Dad had done; leave my memories of David behind? Would I experience the same kind of melancholy as when PK died? I believed neither would happen.

Without David, I might falter like an unanchored boat on an unsettled sea. But I would not founder. He had filled so much of my heart there was no room for despair, much less for another man. And besides, I would do all I could to hold David forever.

◆

David approached me and took my hand, much as Dad had once done when we buried Esther's ashes. That day I had felt alone, isolated by my uncertain feelings. Now David was beside me, walking with me through each twist in the elaborate maze of my emotions.

After a few moments we turned and walked back to the car, then drove toward home in a connected silence.

Many years had passed since I took that dive into uncharted waters, and I reflected on all the times afterwards when we held hands, closed our eyes and took yet another plunge and landed right side up—and still together.

◆

When we pulled into the garage and he cut the engine, I turned to him and said, "Will you marry me?"

He smiled that sweetest of smiles then turned to me. "Are you sure?"

"Absolutely."

"Yes, I'll marry you—again and again, but right here in the garage?"

I laughed, as I had laughed almost daily— through the tough times and the good times of our over thirty years of marriage.

Chapter Twenty-Six

You labored
to leave while struggling
to breathe
again I lay beside you,
and when you inhaled,
I inhaled, too, held the air inside
and tightened my arms around you.

Even though I wholly loved you,
I knew I couldn't hold my breath—
your last breath—forever.
I had no right to even try.

David and I remained married until cancer
claimed his life in 2011. He was 74. Our journey
was a grand adventure I am hugely thankful for
having shared with him.

Of course there were times when dreams
refused to come true; when I felt David took a
detour too far, or he felt he could not make me
happy. But he seldom ceased to surprise me, to
make me laugh and make me feel loved.

Through the years I worked in non-profits
and, sometimes as a writer, briefly again in advertising, and finally as a college teacher—my
most satisfying job. A number of my students
rewarded my faith in them by conquering their

doubts to produce fine books. Those books are my several Nobel Prizes.

And through all those years, hovering close by was the azure balloon. Only now that David is gone has it drifted again just beyond my reach.

◆

I only knowingly lied to David once.

On Friday, February 18, we left the house together for the last time. David endured four hours of chemotherapy. When the oncology nurse examined him, she was concerned because his condition had deteriorated rapidly. She called in the doctor on duty who ordered imaging. That evening, David went through three MRIs, then was taken back to an examining room.

Our grandson, Steven, age twenty-three at the time, was with us that night, the night I finally had to accept that I might lose David. I was consumed by the thought of David leaving me, leaving his children and grandchildren, the world he adventured through and loved, and I could think of little else. So later I asked Steven to tell me what happened that night. Here is what Steven so beautifully and thoughtfully wrote to me:

"That night in the hospital, I was caught up in the moment and piecing together the events and emotions from the past year, the present moment, and coming months all at the same time. There was a lot going on in my head; I can only imagine where your head was.

"When Dr. Lewis came in the room to report the findings of the MRIs, I remember him being direct about the results and what it meant for Grandpa's future. I believe that Grandpa was hoping they would find something that could be fixed and eventually give him back his strength and independence, but, unfortunately, that wasn't the case. I think that's when Grandpa decided the battle you and he were fighting together was going to end sadly either way, and he would rather end it with the greatest amount of 'him' right to the end.

"I think he realized that, if he kept going through treatment after treatment, he was going to become weaker and weaker, and soon might not be the same grandpa, dad, husband we always knew.

"That night, when Dr. Lewis told us that there was little that could be done to improve Grandpa's condition, he suggested a couple of options. He said that, while the treatments may extend grandpa's life, they would probably not improve his quality of life.

"Then Dr. Lewis suggested Grandpa could live the remainder of his life in as much comfort as possible, but this would mean he would pass soon. I remember you trying to explore more options to keep Grandpa with us longer, and that is when Grandpa stopped you and said, 'It's time to talk about what I want.'

"He explained that he thought it was silly to prolong this uncomfortable process with an inevitable end, and that he wanted to live out the rest of his life as himself.

"I'll always remember he held your hand and told you with his witty tone, almost jokingly, that it was his time to go. 'And you're not allowed to come with me,' he said. Grandpa smiled at you to try to cheer you up.

"I remember Dr. Lewis saying that, in the many years he has been working as a doctor, what Grandpa said and how he said it, may have been the most beautiful thing he'd heard.

"It's hard to put all of the memories in words, and I'm sure little pieces will hit me at random times, but I hope this was enough to spark something so you can put it in your words. I'm certainly glad I was there with you and Grandpa that night, and I'm extremely grateful that, right up until the end, Grandpa was the same smart, funny, and loving guy I've always known him to be."

◆

Four days later, as David struggled through the last hours of his life, he raised his head from the pillow and said: "I really don't want to leave you."

I lay down beside him, my hand holding his hand, and said, slowly, deliberately, feeling the full weight of looming tears: "Listen, this is really important."

He nodded, lay back against the pillow and took a labored breath. "I love you with all my being," I said, "and no matter what, you will always be right here, beside me.

"You have given me so much love, so much life. You have taught me so much. You have

264

given me so much of yourself that I feel as if I have nearly become both you and me."

He breathed more peacefully. I lay my head on his shoulder and whispered: "God knows I don't want you to go, but I finally understand why you have to go." I had not yet told the lie.

When I looked at him again, I saw not the fading man next to me, but the spirited, sensitive man who walked into my office some thirty-five years before, the man who said "Wow!" to begin a voyage far beyond what I ever imagined possible.

"My sweet prince."

His breathing slowed, became shallow; his eyes lost their focus. Again, I rested my head against his shoulder. "I am going to be okay," I said.

That was the lie.

With gratitude, appreciation and deep respect
for the worthy people of Nigeria,
who welcomed us with their broad smiles.

And to many generous friends who shared in the
authorship of this work:

Michael Boxall, Joan Casey, Nancy Daugherty,
Linda Durman, Roger Durman, Bob Fiscella, Susan
Fournier, Patty Fowler, Lee Kueser, Carol Sifton,
Dennis Sifton, Muriel Williams, Neil Williams,
Lillian Woolfolk, Susan Wright
who helped me discover what I needed to write
and appeased my qualms along the way.

Phyllis Barber who taught me (again and again)
how to recreate authenticity.

Dalia Liddiard and Ann Cowan who gently guided me
to essential truths by asking all the right questions.

Carol Shaben and Patricia Gray who led me
to an appropriate finale.

Roger Conlee for his remarkably sharp eye.

John Conlee, Kit Fournier, Patricia Gray and Mac Laird
for their many readings, corrections and affirmations
and for their indispensable support as I rediscovered
the joy of writing.

And, especially, with love for our girls:
Beeb, Bub, Tod and Jennie

A portion of the proceeds from this book will be donated to Africare, an African-American organization with effective programs to address the problems of agriculture and food security, health, HIV and AIDS, water, sanitation and the empowerment of women in sub-Saharan Africa.

*Cover photograph by Sarah Kendle
and enhanced by the author*

269

Pre-Publication Acclaim For
Plunge!

"I want to share this book. It is a beautiful read."
— Susan Wright

"The deeply moving scenes drew me into the book and kept me solidly anchored there until setting me free in the most moving scene of all: the ending."
— Mac Laird, author, *Dangerous Differences*.

"A vivid account of love and life in Manhattan and Africa during the 'seventies between two strong and creative soul mates."
—Ann Cowan Buitenhuis, co-founder,
The Canadian Centre for Studies in Publishing

"I didn't want to finish the book. It is exciting; I want it to go on and on and on."
— Dr. Linda Durman

"The poetry is thought-provoking —artistic and yet transparent."
— Muriel Williams

The entire time I read the book (and after), I was filled with great joy and appreciation for love! for life! No small accomplishment. – Carol Lynn Marrazzo, author

"A deeply moving and deeply-felt story which will resonate with others as it resonated with me."
—Michael Boxall, author, *The Great Firewall*

"So well written and so compelling." – Louise Crowley,
Program Director, Vermont College of Fine Arts,
MFA in Writing

271